# Writing Models

## Year 6

## *Pie Corbett*

 **David Fulton** Publishers

*Other titles of interest:*

**Writing Models Year 3**
*Pie Corbett*
ISBN 1-84312-094-1

**Writing Models Year 4**
*Pie Corbett*
ISBN 1-84312-095-X

**Writing Models Year 5**
*Pie Corbett*
ISBN 1-84312-096-8

David Fulton Publishers Ltd
The Chiswick Centre, 414 Chiswick High Road, London W4 5TF

www.fultonpublishers.co.uk

First published in 2004 in Great Britain by David Fulton Publishers

David Fulton Publishers is a division of Granada Learning Limited, part of ITV plc.

*British Library Cataloguing in Publication Data*
A catalogue record for this book is available from the British Library.

ISBN 1-84312-097-6

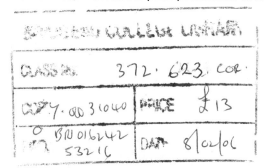

Designed and typeset by Kenneth Burnley, Wirral, Cheshire
Printed and bound in Great Britain

# Contents

# Introduction

**What does the book contain?**

This is part of a series of books for use at Key Stage 2 that contain banks of photocopiable models for writing, covering the full writing range of poetry, fiction and non-fiction for pupils in Years 3–6.

For each text type a complete example has been provided. For some text types, there is also a supplementary extract focusing on a specific aspect of the text type, e.g. openings. Annotated copies of simpler examples provide key teaching points at a glance. There are also simple teachers' notes that give a swift outline of reading and writing activities linked to the examples. To help with differentiation we have included simpler and harder examples.

**How to use the model texts to teach writing**

Writing begins with reading. The more familiar children are with a text type, the more likely it is that they will be able to write in a similar vein. This is because children who read avidly will have internalised the patterns of language. When they come to write, they can then easily slip into the right 'voice' so that what they write 'sounds right'. It is not surprising that the best writers in a class are always children who read. So, any work on writing will always begin with reading plenty of examples.

You also need to provide plenty of opportunities to 'talk the text type', using the same sort of language. For instance, when working on narrative, story-telling helps many children to begin using the appropriate patterns of narrative language. If you are teaching them how to write recounts, then telling anecdotes will get the children into the 'right' voice.

| Written text types | Oral text types |
| --- | --- |
| Narrative | Story-telling |
| Poetry | Poetry performance |
| Recount | Anecdotes |
| Explanation | Explaining |
| Report | Informing |
| Discussion | Debates |
| Persuasion | Arguing a viewpoint |

Ideally, it helps if you can set up something interesting and motivating as a starting point for writing. This may involve first-hand experience, drama, video, music, art, a visit, and so on. Children will be more committed to writing if there is a purpose and some sort of genuine audience. Therefore it helps to publish writing through display, the school website, booklets, photocopied anthologies, etc.

# Introduction

## How to use this book

The models in this book can be turned into OHTs, or photocopied, to use in a variety of ways:

### 1 Analysis

Either as a whole class, in pairs or as individuals, encourage the children to read the text as writers and analyse the structure and language features.

To prepare for writing, look at the specific models provided in this book, analysing how they are structured and what language features are used. The annotated versions and teachers' notes will draw your attention to these. Try to avoid the temptation to tell the children but let them annotate the examples and work out as much as they can for themselves. A problem-solving approach is more likely to embed the learning! This analysis can be turned into a 'writer's toolkit' – a reminder sheet or wall chart that can be used during writing and referred to afterwards for self-evaluation and marking.

Before launching into writing, you may feel that the class needs to practise the spelling of certain key words. For instance, when working on traditional tales, learning how to spell 'once' would be handy! Furthermore, certain specific sentence structures might be needed for the text type you are working on, and these too could be rehearsed. For instance, you could try practising putting together opening lines, or writing sentences beginning 'Suddenly . . .', and so forth. These can be practised on mini-whiteboards. To find ideas for sentence and spelling games, see my book *Jumpstart!*, available from David Fulton.

### 2 Demonstration

You can use the models in this book to demonstrate how to write each of the text types. In the NLS video *Grammar for Writing* you can see teachers holding models in their hands or glancing at a model pinned up beside the board. While writing they talk through their decisions, rehearsing sentences, making alterations and rereading to check for sense and accuracy. When demonstrating, try to ensure that you make specific reference back to the models and the writer's toolkit. Demonstration is useful for any aspect of writing that is new, or that children find difficult. In demonstration, you are able directly to explain and show pupils how to write a text type.

### 3 Shared writing

Demonstration is usually followed by shared composition. Here, you act as scribe for the class or group, leaving them free to focus on the composition. This does not mean accepting any old contribution, but pushing the class to think for themselves and to evaluate their ideas. Weak vocabulary and sentence structure should be challenged. The class may need reminding to return to the model or check the writer's toolkit. In shared composition the teacher scaffolds the pupils' attempts. If children struggle with their own writing, then you will need to keep returning to shared writing, gradually handing over more and more of the decisions to the class.

### 4 Independent writing

Shared writing is usually followed by independent writing. Some children will still find it helpful to have a model to hand for reference as they write. Certainly the model, and the writer's toolkit, can be used for self-evaluation and marking. Some children may need extra support during shared writing – this might be through working with an adult, a partner, using a writing frame, a bank of vocabulary or sentence starters. However, the aim is for the majority to be able to write independently.

Guided writing can be used to teach at the point of writing – to support and challenge. If you find you are stretched for time, it may be more important to use guided time to focus on those who struggle. This means that class teaching can be aimed high.

### 5 Evaluation

After writing, children can self-evaluate. This might be carried out in pairs by using response partners. The author should read through his or her own writing, identifying strengths. He or she can then make selected improvements to the composition – as well as checking on accuracy.

If you are marking the work, try to keep your comments focused, indicating what has worked well and where improvements need to be made:

- Use a highlighter to highlight the best parts.
- Indicate where improvements are needed using symbols such as dotted lines, etc.

When work is returned, pupils should read what the teacher has written, sign it and then be given an opportunity to respond. There should be a range of improvements that each child can make, for example using a more powerful word, improving sentence structure, adding in more information, dropping in a clause, correcting punctuation, improving common spellings, etc. Your marking will also lead the following sessions as it should identify what has to be taught next.

## Using technology

It can be helpful if several children write straight onto blank OHTs. This means that in the plenary, or the next day, these can be used for whole-class teaching – identifying strengths, checking against the models and toolkits and showing how to improve. If you have an interactive whiteboard then a child can compose straight onto the screen. I find it useful if the author will come out, read their own work through and explain what they are pleased with and discuss areas that might need further work. This evidently calls for some sensitive handling, though in the main most children enjoy their chance at the OHP!

## Why use a model?

Sometimes the reading material we use provides an ideal model. For instance, Kit Wright's poem 'Magic Box' works without fail to produce good quality writing. However, most adult writing for children is actually too subtle and complex to offer a model that can easily be imitated. To put it bluntly, Betsy Byars's *The Midnight Fox* may be a great book to use with Year 6 children. But she is a remarkable writer working at level 3,000, and Darren aged 10 years is only at level 2! So, the specific models in this book provide clear structures that will support children's own writing. Those who struggle as writers should stick to imitating the models – while your most able pupils will have already internalised the patterns and should not be hindered from moving beyond.

## Revision

Because of the need to revise all text types and cover story writing thoroughly, I have included models that cover a broad range of writing, which you may well want to use flexibly. In other words, I imagine that teachers may well use some units from term 3 in an earlier term, and so forth.

# Poetry models

## Oakridge Night

The war memorial
sits patiently,
tapping its white stick
in the dark.

Across the park
the trees whisper
in the icy breeze.

The wind sniffs;
leaves chatter their teeth

as the frost dresses
each blade of grass.

A distant siren wails;
streets shrug their shoulders.

The yellow moon smoulders;
bushes yawn before bed;
stars hiss.

Clouds kiss,
then dash home,
on time for once.

*Pie Corbett*

# Poetry models

Choose a place
you know well

# Oakridge Night

The war memorial
sits patiently,
tapping its white stick
in the **dark**.

What can you see?

What is it doing?

Occasional rhymes –
only if they make sense

Across the **park**
the trees **whisper**
in the icy breeze.

Personification

The wind **sniffs**;
leaves **chatter** their teeth

as the frost dresses
each blade of grass.

A distant siren wails;
streets shrug their shoulders.

Think of sounds

Bring 'objects' alive

The yellow moon smoulders;
**b**ushes yawn **b**efore **b**ed;
stars hiss.

Use alliteration

Keep language compressed

Clouds kiss,
then dash home,
on time for once.

Try to find an ending

*Pie Corbett*

# The Day's Eye

The sun rises,
surprises the weary night,
like a sudden joke.
Daylight.

The sun gleams,
beams kindly heat
like an oven's plate.
Streets sweat.

The sun sneaks,
peeks through misty cloud,
like a sly thief,
alone in a crowd.

The sun sleeps,
creeps into cool shade,
like a honey cat.
Shadows fade.

The sun slips,
dips into night,
like a closing mouth,
swallowing light.

*Pie Corbett*

# What Am I?

I dig deep,
Shooting down
Into darkness.

I tunnel,
Creating routes
Into earth.

I reach high,
Branching out,
Into light.

I uncurl,
Leaving green
Into sun.

I grow,
Barking silently
Into life.

*Pie Corbett*

TERM 2: **POEMS IN DIFFERENT FORMS: RIDDLES**
(Easier)

# What Am I?

Typical riddle title

Alliteration

I **d**ig deep,
**Shoot**ing down
Into darkness.

Play on words
('shoots' of a plant)

I tunnel,
Creating routes
**Into** earth.

First line: use 'I' and
powerful verb

Third line: use
'Into'

I reach high,
**Branching** out,
Into light.

Play on words

I uncurl,
**Leaving** green
Into sun.

Play on words

I grow,
**Barking** silently
Into life.

Play on words

Contrasting ideas

*Pie Corbett*

# Who Am I?

Like a midnight, masked **b**andit on the prowl,

snuffling through hedges, r**a**iding the lawn.

Weary worm-**d**igger, up before dawn –

like a **g**hostly thief, friend of fox and owl

A moonlit intrud**e**r, foul fiend of the dark.

I blunder on, bearing my zeb**r**a mask.

# Seasonal Haiku

Wintry night.
Carols drift down King Street.
A necklace of lights on the dark throat of night.

December morning.
On the doorstep, frosted bottles.
Inside, we crunch toast.

April showers –
Clouds are sly cats.
The sun plays tag.

Spring afternoon.
At the roadside, fist of daffodils.
Cars snarl on the motorway.

Summer night.
A radio plays too loud.
Swallows skim the road.

The first Holiday.
Church bells blossom.
The fat sun warms our street.

Autumn breeze.
Leaves curl.
The toad sleeps like a stone.

November bonfires.
Stars freckle the night.
The moon is a silver boat.

*Pie Corbett*

# Poetry models

## Seasonal Haiku

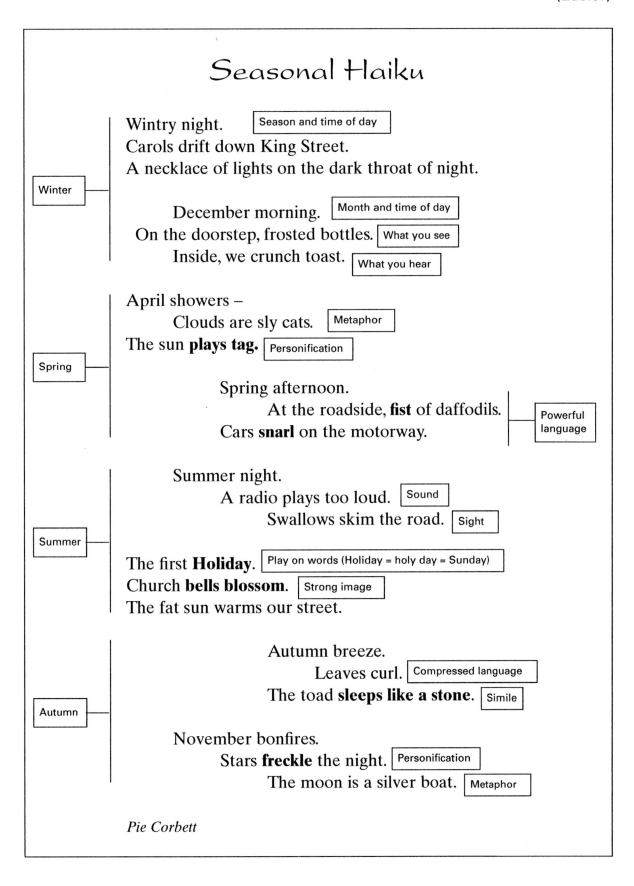

**Winter**

Wintry night. [Season and time of day]
Carols drift down King Street.
A necklace of lights on the dark throat of night.

December morning. [Month and time of day]
On the doorstep, frosted bottles. [What you see]
Inside, we crunch toast. [What you hear]

**Spring**

April showers –
Clouds are sly cats. [Metaphor]
The sun **plays tag.** [Personification]

Spring afternoon.
At the roadside, **fist** of daffodils. [Powerful language]
Cars **snarl** on the motorway.

**Summer**

Summer night.
A radio plays too loud. [Sound]
Swallows skim the road. [Sight]

The first **Holiday**. [Play on words (Holiday = holy day = Sunday)]
Church **bells blossom**. [Strong image]
The fat sun warms our street.

**Autumn**

Autumn breeze.
Leaves curl. [Compressed language]
The toad **sleeps like a stone**. [Simile]

November bonfires.
Stars **freckle** the night. [Personification]
The moon is a silver boat. [Metaphor]

*Pie Corbett*

9

# Holiday Haiku

The heat beats down;
ants file past in a ragged line;
distant hills shiver.


Like human bells –
voices ring – while wind wrinkles
the pool's cool skin.


Loafing on the patio.
Flies dodge each blow –
busy slapping myself.


Beneath the porch light
a gecko waits;
to welcome us home.


The moon edges
a slice over the mountain –
then floats up
like a great balloon.


Bats dither.
Cicadas whir.
Sleep is impossible.

*Pie Corbett*

# An Odd Kettle of Fish

The detectives said that
the books had been cooked.
(They tasted good.)

My teacher said we could
have a free hand.
(I added it to my collection.)

Some people bottle up
their feelings.
(I keep mine in a jar.)

My Mother said –
'Hold your tongue!'
(It was too slippery.)

When my sister laughs
she drives me round the bend.
(I catch the bus back.)

Dad told me
to keep a stiff upper lip.
(It's in a box by my bed.)

My Uncle is a terrible
name-dropper.
(I help my Aunty to sweep them up.)

In the school races
I licked everyone in the class.
(It made my tongue sore.)

*Pie Corbett*

# An Odd Kettle of Fish

Use everyday sayings

The detectives said that
the books had been cooked.
(They tasted good.)

My teacher said we could
have a free hand.
(I added it to my collection.)

Take saying literally

Some people bottle up
their feelings.
(I keep mine in a jar.)

Quote people

My Mother said –
'Hold your tongue!'
(It was too slippery.)

Quote people

When my sister laughs
she drives me round the bend.
(I catch the bus back.)

Quote people

Dad told me
to keep a stiff upper lip.
(It's in a box by my bed.)

Use simple three-line pattern

My Uncle is a terrible
name-dropper.
(I help my Aunty to sweep them up.)

Notice what people say

In the school races
I licked everyone in the class.
(It made my tongue sore.)

*Pie Corbett*

TERM 2: **POEMS IN DIFFERENT FORMS: USING EVERYDAY SAYINGS**
(Harder)

# The Poem Imagines it is a Horror Film

He was so afraid that
He had his heart in his mouth.
(Bloodstains covered his tie.)

It was so funny that
She laughed her head off.
(They couldn't stitch it back on.)

'Don't look a gift horse in the mouth,'
I was told at school.
(They bite.)

I hit the nail on the head.
(It screamed with pain.)

I was so angry
That it made my blood boil.
(My brains cooked nicely.)

When she lied
I saw right through her.
(The hole in her head bled.)

My heart sank into my boots.
(The blood warmed my feet.)

It's not fair –
My teacher keeps
Jumping down my throat.
(It makes it hard to breeeeeeeathe.)

*Pie Corbett*

# Things to do Around Oakridge

Skateboard by the rec   race each other up and down the laggers.
Wait for the valley to turn green   hide in the fog.
Hoot like owls   buy sweets at the shop.
Be the first to hear the cuckoo.

Stay up late   when the summer heat makes sleep impossible.
watch the badgers eating bread and milk next door.
Look at owls in the lane   swooping low over fields.
Kick a ball about   swing high.

Pick blackberries   get stained fingers.
Kick through leaves   chase imaginary ghosts down dark lanes.
Look at the stained glass window glowing at night.
Watch and wait   for UFOs   across the valley.

Throw snowballs   slide down Strawberry Banks on bin liners.
Knock icicles off the school roof   skid on the road.
Drink hot tea outside   and watch your breath.
Smell woodsmoke   drifting across the village.

*Pie Corbett*

# Poetry models

| Use your own locality | **Things to do Around Oakridge** | |

Skateboard by the rec   race each other up and down the **laggers.**   `Alleyways`
Wait for the valley to turn green   hide in the fog.
Hoot like owls   buy sweets at the shop.
Be the first to hear the cuckoo.

*Spring things to do*

Stay up late   when the summer heat makes sleep impossible.   `List real things that you do`
watch the badgers eating bread and milk next door.
Look at owls in the lane   swooping low over fields.
Kick a ball about   swing high.

*Summer events*

Pick blackberries   get stained fingers.
Kick through leaves   chase imaginary ghosts **down dark** lanes.   `Alliteration`
Look at the stained glass window glowing at night.   `Stretch lines with spaces`
Watch and wait   for UFOs   across the valley.

*Autumn happenings*

Throw snowballs   slide down Strawberry Banks on bin liners.   `Keep language compressed`
Knock icicles off the school roof   **skid on the road.**
Drink hot tea outside   and watch your breath.
Smell woodsmoke   drifting across the village.

*Winter time*

*Pie Corbett*

15

# It's Early

It's early –
The stars are frosted flowers
And the night a velvet mole.

It's early –
The postman's whistle
Surprises the dark
Like a waking spell.

It's early –
Dogs bark back a greeting.
Cats arch and purr.

It's early –
In bedrooms the sleepy stir.
Blackbirds are hedgerow alarms.

It's early –
Dreams are a fading ferris wheel
That spins past too fast.

It's early –
The day waits patiently for you
To rise at last.

*Pie Corbett*

# Spanish Holiday

A lone cloud
      above mountain tops
         sidles by.
         It's getting late.
Swallows anchored
        to the blue.


Night swim – moon crumbles – stars scatter.


The moon
      sneaks a peak
over the mountain's shoulder
     and cheekily winks.


      Cicadas stop buzzing.
I wake –
        the silence deafens me.


The outside shower drips,
     taps a steady beat –
wasps settle to sip.


     Stunned by sun.
Heat bounces off white walls.
     A lizard agrees.

Clouds      drift      my thoughts

Just round the mountain bend,
        the village leaps into view.
White houses cling on.

      On the mountain track,
        we stop
to eat mulberries –
        blood-red juice
stains our thieving hands.

Down donkey tracks
      we plod,
stop beneath a fig tree,
      stoop for shade.
Three cats splayed
      in the shadows;
      a dog just
        raises its head
      in greeting.

Two sparrows tussle
        over breadcrumbs –
we sip black, iced coffee.

*Pie Corbett*

TERM 3: **SHORT POEM SEQUENCE**
(Easier)

# Spanish Holiday

Vary the line length and pattern

A lone cloud
    above mountain tops
        sidles by.
        It's getting late.
Swallows anchored    What can you see?
        to the blue.

Watery reflections

Night swim – moon crumbles – stars scatter.

Internal rhymes

The moon
    **sneaks** a **peak**
over the mountain's shoulder
    and **cheekily** winks.

    Cicadas stop buzzing.   What can you hear?
I wake –
        the silence deafens me.   Contradictory idea

The outside shower drips,
    taps a steady beat –   Sounds echo meaning
wasps settle to sip.

    Stunned by sun.   Only use rhyme if it makes good sense
Heat bounces off white walls.
    A lizard agrees.

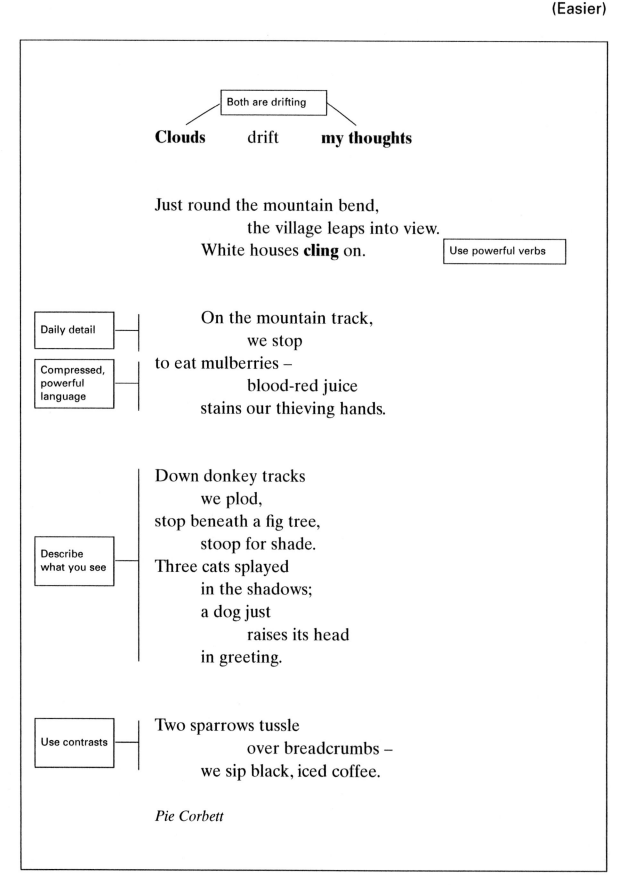

Both are drifting

**Clouds**    drift    **my thoughts**

Just round the mountain bend,
        the village leaps into view.
White houses **cling** on.

Use powerful verbs

Daily detail

On the mountain track,
        we stop
to eat mulberries –
        blood-red juice
stains our thieving hands.

Compressed,
powerful
language

Describe
what you see

Down donkey tracks
        we plod,
stop beneath a fig tree,
        stoop for shade.
Three cats splayed
        in the shadows;
        a dog just
                raises its head
        in greeting.

Use contrasts

Two sparrows tussle
        over breadcrumbs –
we sip black, iced coffee.

*Pie Corbett*

# South of France – Holiday Creatures

Crazy ants,
Fuss by the pool –
on a mission
to nowhere.

On the balcony –
a black lizard
scuttles up the wall –
pauses, poses,
performs for us all.

In the valley
a hawk hangs in
the sultry heat;
an anchor lost;
a sea of sky.

An old cat ambles by;
it sits like a fat Buddha
at the top of the steps
to contemplate the flowers.

Bees busy;
butterflies
dizzy past.

Further up the valley,
grunting like piglets,
two frogs gossip
about the
moon's dumb
face.

*Tuesday 17 April 2001*

# Fiction models

## Diving for the Brick

I stood at the side of the pool. The water was quite still and I could see the bottom. Mr Gatenby stood with his arms folded, shouting at the class.

It was so cold that I had goose-bumps up and down my arms. My legs were shaking and my teeth had begun to chatter. Petie's lips looked blue. It was raining a light drizzle. Icily, the wind blew.

Swimming. I lived in fear of Friday morning. Whatever the weather, Mr Gatenby would march us down to the school's pride and joy – the new outdoor school pool. It was all right for him, dressed in his tracksuit and pumps.

Already, I could feel my chest tightening, and the familiar rasp as the asthma took hold. I tried to calm myself down, steadying each breath but the more I tried, the harder it seemed.

'Stop gulping like a fish,' snapped Mr Gatenby, staring at me. He was holding a brick.

'This is what you are diving for,' he went on, 'you swim straight down, grab hold of it and swim straight up. It's easy enough. Who wants to go first?' He eyeballed the queue. There was a steely silence. Everyone shuffled and looked elsewhere.

I gazed into the water and tried to imagine what it would be like diving that far down. Supposing I reached the bottom and then hadn't enough air to get back up? My chest felt compressed, as if an iron band had been placed across it and was being steadily tightened. Anxiously, Petie glanced at me. He could hear each wheeze.

I knew what was coming. I could feel Mr Gatenby's eyes upon me.

'You!' He was pointing at me. It was no good arguing. I'd tried that before. 'Exercise,' he'd told me. 'That's what you need. Exercise to toughen you up. You're a feeble specimen.' And I was. The smallest boy in the class, puny arms, no muscles and a chest that seemed to go in rather than out. I had ribs that poked out like a xylophone.

He lobbed the brick into the pool. We all watched it wriggle down, the water echoing out from the splash. It hit the bottom, seemed to shimmer and then the water began to still.

I stood on the edge; my heart thumping. Then, without really thinking about what I was doing, I jumped in, legs first. The cold shock seemed to make the world stop. I flailed my arms and broke the surface. I could hear Mr Gatenby shouting at me to dive back down.

So, I leaned forwards and peered through the water, just making out the shape of the brick. Then, rasping in a breath, I plunged down, kicking my legs as hard as I could. I kept my eyes open and as I sunk deeper, the shouts faded to echoes. I lost the world above as it became a distant shape of light. My whole being was now aimed at that brick.

My chest tightened, my heart raced. It was getting harder and harder, the deeper I went. My ears began to buzz. The water seemed to be pressing in on me. The deeper I went, the colder and darker it became. I could feel the distance between the surface and myself, gathering.

Then my hand touched the rough edge of the brick. I kicked once more, grabbed it and struggled round to swim upwards. I thrust as hard as I could, but by now my legs only fluttered weakly. My face surged through a sudden rush of bubbles. My lungs ached.

The brick weighed heavy, tugging me back, pulling my hand down. But still my body managed to shoot up through a blur of water, as if propelled by some unseen force.

I broke the surface and spluttered. Hands reached down and pulled me up like a dead fish, dragged over the side of the pool.

I sat there, hunched up, nursing the brick, coughing and spluttering as my chest wheezed and whistled like an old man. The class crowded round, cheering, patting me on the back. And as I struggled to catch each breath, and my body heaved, silence fell. Quietly, as if they were one person, they all turned and looked accusingly across the pool.

Curious, I too looked up. Through a jumble of legs, I caught a glimpse of Mr Gatenby. He was on the other side of the pool, standing with his arms folded just looking at us. And it struck me how lonely he looked.

# Diving for the Brick

I stood on the side of the pool. The water was quite still and I could see the bottom. Mr Gatenby stood with his arms folded, **shouting at the class**.

It was so cold that I had goose-bumps up and down my arms. My legs were shaking and my teeth had begun to chatter. Petie's lips looked blue. It was raining a light drizzle. **Icily**, the wind blew.

Swimming. I lived in fear of Friday morning. Whatever the weather, Mr Gatenby would march us down to the school's pride and joy – the new outdoor school pool. It was all right for him, dressed in his tracksuit and pumps.

Already, I could feel my chest tightening, and the familiar rasp as the asthma took hold. I tried to calm myself down, steadying each breath but the more I tried, the harder it seemed.

'Stop gulping like a fish,' snapped Mr Gatenby, **staring at me**. He was holding a brick.

'This is what you are diving for,' he went on, 'you swim straight down, grab hold of it and swim straight up. It's easy enough. Who wants to go first?' He eyeballed the queue. There was a steely silence. Everyone shuffled and looked elsewhere.

I gazed into the water and tried to imagine what it would be like diving that far down. Supposing I reached the bottom and then hadn't enough air to get back up? My chest felt compressed, as if an iron band had been placed across it and was being steadily tightened. **Anxiously**, Petie glanced at me. He could hear each wheeze.

I knew what was coming. I could feel Mr Gatenby's eyes upon me.

'You!' He was pointing at me. It was no good arguing. I'd tried that before. 'Exercise,' he'd told me. 'That's what you need. Exercise to toughen you up. You're a feeble specimen.' And I was. The smallest boy in the class, puny arms, no muscles and a chest that seemed to go in rather than out. I had ribs that poked out like a xylophone.

## Side annotations

**Opening that visually sets the scene**

**Build-up**

**Dilemma**

**Add on an '-ing' clause to show what someone is doing**

**Adverb starter**

**Establishes the character's fear (the monster)**

**Add on a supporting action after speech**

**Keep dialogue limited**

**Reveal main character's thoughts**

**Adverb starter for emphasis**

**Background information**

# Fiction models

He **lobbed** the brick into the pool. We all **watched** it **wriggle** down, the water **echoing** out from the splash. It **hit** the bottom, seemed to **shimmer** and then the water began to **still**.

*Use powerful verbs*

I stood on the edge; my heart thumping. Then, without really thinking about what I was doing, I jumped in, legs first. The cold shock seemed to make the world stop. I flailed my arms and broke the surface. I could hear Mr Gatenby shouting at me to dive back down.

*Deepening the dilemma*

**So**, I leaned forwards and peered through the water, just making out the shape of the brick. **Then**, rasping in a breath, I plunged down, kicking my legs as hard as I could. I kept my eyes open and as I sunk deeper, the shouts faded to echoes. I lost the world above as it became a distant shape of light. My whole being was now aimed at that brick.

*Use connectives to move the action forward*

My chest tightened, my heart raced. It was getting harder and harder, the deeper I went. **My ears began to buzz.** The water seemed to be pressing in on me. The deeper I went, the colder and darker it became. I could feel the distance between the surface and myself, gathering.

*Vary sentence length for impact*

Then my hand touched the rough edge of the brick. I kicked once more, grabbed it and struggled round to swim upwards. I thrust as hard as I could, but by now my legs only fluttered weakly. My face surged through a sudden rush of bubbles. **My lungs ached.**

*Short sentences are good for paragraph endings*

*Resolution*

The brick weighed heavy, **tugging me back, pulling my hand down.** But still my body managed to shoot up through a blur of water, as if propelled by some unseen force.

*Add on '-ing' clause*

*Use similes to build pictures*

I broke the surface and spluttered. Hands reached down and pulled me up **like a dead fish**, dragged over the side of the pool.

I sat there, **hunched** up, **nursing** the brick, **coughing** and **spluttering** as my chest wheezed and whistled like an old man. The class crowded round, cheering, patting me on the back. And as I struggled to catch each breath, and my body heaved, silence fell. **Quietly**, as if they were one person, they all turned and looked accusingly across the pool.

*Use powerful verbs to show how a character feels*

*Ending – showing character change*

*Adverb starter*

Curious, I too looked up. Through a jumble of legs, I caught a glimpse of Mr Gatenby. He was on the other side of the pool, standing with his arms folded just looking at us. **And it struck me how lonely he looked.**

*Try to end with a punch!*

# Double Dare

Connor dreamed about falling. Some nights he didn't want to go to sleep because he knew that the dream would come. In it, he was standing on the top of a tall building. It was so tall that you couldn't see the bottom. And even though he did not want to, something would drag him to the edge and then he would be falling. Not flying, but falling. Downwards, with a sudden lurch of fear in his stomach.

Some nights he could wake himself, force himself up out of the dream. He'd wake in a panic, heart thudding, feeling hot and sweaty with the sheets tangled up where he had been struggling.

No one at school knew about Connor's fear of heights. And that was the way he intended to keep it. He was quite happy. Year 6, and SATs under his belt. The last half of the summer term, and the class were all enjoying themselves. Mr Moses had fixed a brilliant day out and they were piled in the coach, on the last leg home, when it broke down.

But it didn't matter. They had broken down in the South Downs, and the coach had pulled in by an old quarry. Mr Moses had told them to stay close while he waited with the driver and Miss Davies for the 'rescue team'. They knew that he fancied Miss Davies so they ran off and hid nearby, to watch them chatting by the coach. Bazzer reckoned that if they waited long enough they'd see some action. After all, Miss Davies was cute with long blonde hair and very pretty. You couldn't miss it.

The girls told the boys to grow up and went off moodily to pick flowers and look at birds . . . soon everyone else got bored. Moses wasn't making any interesting moves and obviously needed to be bought *The Beginner's Book of Chatting Up* for a leaver's present. The class wandered off to inspect the quarry.

Connor didn't know who started it but the next thing he knew someone had dared everyone else to climb the quarry. Immediately, his heart began to race and his fear clutched at his stomach. He could feel the sickening bite as worry gnawed away at him like a rat.

'Supposing the coach gets going, Moses will kill us,' he muttered. But it was no good.

'Double dare, Connor,' yelled Dabber. 'First to the top.' He leaped at the edge of the quarry as if he was attacking it and began to scrabble up. Everyone else crowded round, chanting and clapping their hands. The sound of their voices echoed round the quarry, 'Double dare, double dare.'

But Connor stood firm, unable to move, as Dabber scrambled higher.

'You scared or what,' said Yogi, pressing his face too close.

'If that idiot wants to spend his time climbing up, that's his business. But I'm not getting in trouble with Moses on his behalf,' said Connor. The others looked at him and he could see them muttering to each other. He could guess what they were saying.

Everyone was watching as Dabber went higher and higher. By now he was nearing the top and looked no more than an ant on the upper part of the chalk face of the quarry. But just before he reached the top, he seemed to pause. Then he slid, sending a flurry of chalk and stones flying down. Then he was quite still, clinging onto the face, not daring to move. His voice echoed down.

'I'm stuck,' he yelled. They could all hear the tremor, the catch of fear.

'Blimey, Moses will kill us,' said Lonny. Everyone started talking at once. Some reckoned he'd only got a few minutes left. Others thought he'd pull himself together. No one suggested the sensible thing – getting Mr Moses.

Then they heard the sound of Dabber crying. It came in short, sharp stabs. Connor could imagine what Dabber was feeling; the way the fear was washing over him in a cold wave that would paralyse any movement. He also knew what he had to do. Without thinking, he began to climb. Fiona ran forwards and grabbed his arm. 'Don't do it, I'll get Moses,' but Connor shook his head.

'I'll be all right,' he replied, trying to sound confident. But their eyes met and he knew that she had seen the sudden flash of fear. She stepped back and he climbed on and up.

Connor used the little tufts of grass that grew on the chalk surface as handholds. Carefully, he used the stones that jutted out as handholds. It was steep and he knew that it would be fatal if he looked down. So, he concentrated on moving up, pausing every now and then to glance at Dabber.

About ten minutes later, he reached him. Connor dared not look down, as he knew that if he did, they would both be stuck there, frozen in fear like two flies, stuck for ever on the edge of the world.

'It's me Dabber,' he said softly. 'Let's do the last bit together.'

'I'll fall,' snapped Dabber. He was rigid and unable to move. Connor began to talk slowly and softly to relax Dabber. Then he suggested a movement and bit-by-bit he managed to help him on and up. Sometimes he had to find Dabber a foothold, actually holding his foot as he moved. What frightened Connor most was the thought that he might catch Dabber's fear like some sort of quick-fire disease.

TERM 1: **NARRATIVE: DEFEATING THE MONSTER**
(Harder)

The top came suddenly. The grass poked over the edge like an unruly haircut. The two boys dragged themselves over the lip of the cliff and lay on the grass panting. Connor could feel his legs shaking.

'Thanks,' stammered Dabber, as Connor stood up. For the first time, Connor looked back over the edge and down. He could see the road and the garage team mending the coach like miniature models. Far below, he could see the class watching. He waved and he heard their cheers. Right at the front of the group, he could see Fiona standing on her own, waving to him. It was like looking at a map that was real. He could see for miles, the fields set out like miniature handkerchiefs and the tiny roads winding across the landscape.

Connor and Dabber trudged back down the lane that led to the road. They said nothing to each other. It had been a double dare and Connor had fulfilled his pledge. A double dare could not be refused.

But more than that. When he slept that night, the dream came back. Once again, he was on top of the same building with his feet curled on the very edge. Then he was leaning ever increasingly forwards, till he began to fall. Only this time, he noticed that he had spread his arms out on each side, like a large cross. And he was not falling – not falling – but flying. For Connor had found his wings.

---

# Break-in

She watched from the side gate as they left the building. There were three of them. Jules pressed back into the hedge and kept as still as possible. She could feel a thorn digging into her side.

A moment later, they were down the path and off up the road. The kid was running on ahead and his mother kept shouting at him. Typical parents, thought Jules. Always bossing others about.

She waited a few seconds longer and then could resist it no longer. She slipped the latch on the side gate, walked straight up to the kitchen door and the next moment she was inside. The warmth of the kitchen engulfed her. Her skin prickled with goose bumps.

She stood still for a moment, closed her eyes and just breathed in the warmth, the homely smells. She could hear the clock ticking, the central heating whirring. And she could smell coffee.

Idle brutes, she thought. They hadn't even bothered to clear anything away. It was like the *Mary Celeste*. Coffee cups on the table, not a drop touched. They were steaming hot too, but Jules had been cold for so long that she didn't mind. She piled in three sugars and took a swig from the largest mug.

It burnt her tongue and she could feel the heat flood through her body. It was too hot but the warmth revived her ... maybe the smaller mug would be easier to drink ...

## TERM 1: **NARRATIVE: A MODERN RETELLING FROM ONE VIEWPOINT**
(Easier)

# Break-in

| Dramatic, mysterious opening |

She watched from the side gate as they left the building. There were three of them. Jules pressed back into the hedge and kept as still as possible. She could feel a thorn digging into her side.

A moment later, they were down the path and off up the road. The kid was running on ahead and his mother kept shouting at him. **Typical parents, thought Jules. Always bossing others about.**

| Reveal the main character's thoughts |

She waited a few seconds longer and then could resist it no longer. **She slipped the latch on the side gate, walked straight up to the kitchen door and the next moment she was inside.** The warmth of the kitchen engulfed her. Her skin prickled with goose bumps.

| Use a sentence of three events to speed up action |

| Keep paragraphs short |

She stood still for a moment, closed her eyes and just breathed in the warmth, the homely smells. She could hear the clock ticking, the central heating whirring. And she could smell coffee.

| Use the senses to build the setting for the reader |

**Idle brutes, she thought. They hadn't even bothered to clear anything away.** It was like the *Mary Celeste*. Coffee cups on the table, not a drop touched. They were steaming hot too, but Jules had been cold for so long that she didn't mind. She piled in three sugars and took a swig from the largest mug.

| Show the character's thoughts or feelings |

It burnt her tongue and she could feel the heat flood through her body. It was too hot but the warmth revived her . . . maybe the smaller mug would be easier to drink . . .

| You do not always have to retell the whole tale |

# Bird Attack

Mr Jenkins was upstairs fiddling about with his computer. It annoyed his wife something rotten, but he didn't care. Selfish. That was what she'd told him. He smiled to himself, turned the radio higher in case she called him and booted up the computer. He had only just discovered a new games website and was keen to get back on. He was in the middle of a game of Zorax with several other players and had agreed to log on at six o'clock.

Downstairs, Mrs Jenkins stared at the pile of ironing in the kitchen corner. It seemed to grow of its own accord, she thought. It almost had a life of its own. She stood by the ironing board and waited for the iron to warm up. Once the steam hissed, she began to iron, smoothing down the creases, straightening the lines in the trousers and shirts. There was something therapeutic about iron-ing out the wrinkles, she thought. Like smoothing away your problems. She could hear her husband's chair creaking and the radio thudding out music.

Out in the garden, Sally was hanging out yet more washing. It was her only real job around the house and she didn't mind helping Mum all that much. What she did mind was that it was always her. Her brother Simon never did anything to help. It was always the same. Mum would ask and Simon would refuse – point blank. It

## TERM 1: **NARRATIVE: A MODERN RETELLING FROM ONE VIEWPOINT**
(Harder)

always ended with Sally taking on Simon's jobs. She felt guilty watching her Mum.

Sal glanced up at the birds on the telegraph wires. There was a long line of black birds, sitting silently, just watching her. She shuddered, even though it was not cold. She felt sure that they were watching her. Silly girl, she thought, shaking her head. Even so, she began to work just that little bit quicker, watching the birds out of the corner of her eye as she did . . .

# 50-word Mini-sagas

Once upon a time there were three goats that wanted to cross a bridge to get to some grass on the other side. A bad-tempered troll tried to stop them but the largest goat knocked him into the water.

In the night the beans grew up to the sky. Next morning Jack climbed up and robbed the giant of his talking harp and golden goose. The goose laid golden eggs so they moved to a better neighbourhood!

'No way, you stay at home!' But a fairy appeared and Cinderella went to the ball. At midnight, she dashed home. The glass slipper she left behind was the prince's only clue to her identity. Luckily the slipper did not fit the Ugly Sisters. It fitted Cinderella. Wedding bells rang.

'I'm so hungry, so weary.' She lay down and slept, leaving behind her a trail of destruction. Later that morning, the three owners returned.

His mother had warned him often enough but he never listened. All it took was a puff of wind to unbalance him. From the town wall, he fell. The passers-by tried their best but it was no good.

# 50-word Mini-sagas

| Billy Goats Gruff | Once upon a time there were three goats that wanted to cross a bridge to get to some grass on the other side. A bad-tempered troll tried to stop them but the largest goat knocked him into the water. | Straightforward retelling with all details missed out |

| Jack and the Beanstalk | In the night the beans grew up to the sky. Next morning Jack climbed up and robbed the giant of his talking harp and golden goose. The goose laid golden eggs so they moved to a better neighbourhood! | Retelling with some gaps for the reader to fill in |

| Cinderella | 'No way, you stay at home!' But a fairy appeared and Cinderella went to the ball. At midnight, she dashed home. The glass slipper she left behind was the prince's only clue to her identity. Luckily the slipper did not fit the Ugly Sisters. It fitted Cinderella. Wedding bells rang. | Start at the key moment – omit background detail |

| Goldilocks and the Three Bears | 'I'm so hungry, so weary.' She lay down and slept, leaving behind her a trail of destruction. Later that morning, the three owners returned. | Very little detail – focus on the most dramatic moment |

| Humpty Dumpty | His mother had warned him often enough but he never listened. All it took was a puff of wind to unbalance him. From the town wall, he fell. The passers-by tried their best but it was no good. | Retelling a nursery rhyme |

# Three Bears

Mother Bear    Will you put that Gameboy down and come and eat your porridge?

Baby Bear    Oh Mum, do I have to?

Mother Bear    Yes. And that is final. I'm not saying it twice.

Baby Bear    (*reluctantly*) OK Mum.

Mother Bear    And don't think that doesn't apply to you.
(*looking at Father Bear*) Your porridge is ready as well.

Baby Bear    (*whining*) But it's too hot Mum.

Mother Bear    Well blow on it then. Go on, pretend you're Mr Wolf.
Give it a good puff!

Father Bear    This is too hot. Let's leave it to cool down. Come on, let's stretch our legs while it cools off. A walk would do us some good – knock off a few pounds!

Mother Bear    (*as they leave*) Aren't you going to lock up?

Father Bear    (*off stage*) We won't be long. No one's about this time of morning anyway. Honestly, you fuss too much.

Mother Bear    You'll be sorry one day. Just you wait and see.

# Fiction models

# Three Bears

| | | |
|---|---|---|
| Notice conventions of layout | Mother Bear | Will you put that **Gameboy** down and come and eat your porridge? |

Use modern references in traditional tale for humour

Use what characters say to reflect their feelings

| | |
|---|---|
| Baby Bear | Oh Mum, do I have to? |
| Mother Bear | Yes. And that is final. I'm not saying it twice. |

Note use of italics for instructions to actor

| | |
|---|---|
| Baby Bear | (*reluctantly*) OK Mum. |
| Mother Bear | And don't think that doesn't apply to you. (*looking at Father Bear*) Your porridge is ready as well. |

Do not overdo instructions

| | |
|---|---|
| Baby Bear | (*whining*) But it's too hot Mum. |
| Mother Bear | Well blow on it then. Go on, pretend you're Mr Wolf. Give it a good puff! |

Refer to other tales

| | |
|---|---|
| Father Bear | This is too hot. Let's leave it to cool down. Come on, let's stretch our legs while it cools off. A walk would do us some good – **knock off a few pounds!** |

Making dialogue sound modern

Stage directions

| | |
|---|---|
| Mother Bear | (*as they leave*) Aren't you going to lock up? |
| Father Bear | (*off stage*) We won't be long. No one's about this time of morning anyway. Honestly, you fuss too much. |
| Mother Bear | You'll be sorry one day. Just you wait and see. |

Introducing notion of what might happen

# Jack and the High-Rise Block of Flats

Mother   Your report is a disgrace. It's the same in every subject. They all say the same. Idle. Work not done, or handed in late. Nothing but a pack of excuses. Well, what have you got to say for yourself then?

Jack   (*grunts*) Mmmm.

Mother   You're just like your father. That's the trouble. He was an idle so-and-so. If you don't get up and do some work, I'm throwing you out on your ear. Do you understand?

Jack   (*getting up from the floor where he has been sleeping – yawns and stretches*) OK, OK – so what do you want me to do?

Mother   Well, we're so poor that we need some money desperately. I don't like doing this but we've no alternative.

Jack   Doing what?

Mother   Take old Daisy down to the market and make sure that you get a good price.

Jack   If you say so, Mother.

Mother   I do say so – and what is more, I want all the cash. You
are not to spend any of it on the way back. Do you understand? The roof is leaking, the windows swing in the wind
and there is no wood to stoke the fire. We've only a few
old potatoes left to eat . . . I want a good price for Daisy –
or we'll be the ones chewing grass . . .

# Evaluation of Skellig

When I reached the end of *Skellig*, I didn't want it to end. In fact, towards the end I slowed down reading so I could savour each moment.

My favourite part of the novel is when Skellig visits the baby in hospital. This happens in a dream sequence and it brings Michael and his Mum close together at the end of the novel.

The main characters are really well portrayed. I like Mina because she is a free spirit. Of course, Skellig is interesting because he is a sort of angel. He is like a wounded angel that has been blown off course somewhere along the line.

I found that the setting was very powerful because David Almond described it really clearly using all the senses – especially the garage where Michael finds Skellig. I found it easy to see Michael clambering over piles of dusty stuff and then finding this strange shape right at the back. It was quite frightening.

The most dramatic moment in the book was when Michael, Mina and Skellig dance together. As they moved round and round, it reminded me of stirring a magic potion because out of the dance Skellig is set free and he is able to save the baby. This would really look good on stage as I could see it in my mind. I love the idea that we might all have once had wings.

I would recommend this book for anyone over nine years. It is one of my favourite books at the moment because it is magical and mysterious.

# Evaluation of Skellig

**When I reached the end of** *Skellig*, I didn't want it to end. In fact, towards the end I slowed down reading so I could savour each moment.

> Refer to *how* you read

**My favourite part of the novel is** when Skellig visits the baby in hospital. This happens in a dream sequence and it brings Michael and his Mum close together at the end of the novel.

> Try to interpret

**The main characters are** really well portrayed. **I like** Mina because she is a free spirit. Of course, Skellig is interesting because he is a sort of angel. He is like a wounded angel that has been blown off course somewhere along the line.

> Give your own ideas

> Use paragraph openings to organise your comments on the text

**I found that the setting** was very powerful because David Almond described it really clearly using all the senses – especially the garage where Michael finds Skellig. I found it easy to see Michael clambering over piles of dusty stuff and then finding this strange shape right at the back. It was quite frightening.

> When thinking about setting, remember what made a strong visual impression

> How did you feel?

**The most dramatic moment in the book was** when Michael, Mina and Skellig dance together. As they moved round and round, it reminded me of stirring a magic potion because out of the dance Skellig is set free and he is able to save the baby. This would really look good on stage as I could see it in my mind. I love the idea that we might all have once had wings.

> Try to make connections

**I would recommend this book** for anyone over nine years. It is one of my favourite books at the moment because it is magical and mysterious.

> Give reasons. Adding quotes would make this even better

# Kissing the Railings

'Do you always do what your brothers tell you? Supposing they told you to jump off a bridge, I suppose you'd do that?' Kim had heard it often enough but it wasn't easy being the youngest of five. She was always the one to be caught, the one to fall over and hurt herself.

That morning they had awoken to a world of white. The High Street traffic was at a standstill. The streets seemed eerily silent. Even the birds were not up to much. Sparrows hunched on telegraph wires, their feathers puffed up to keep them warm.

They left for school early, straggling down the road, kicking at icy puddles, sliding on the pavement. Kim kept to the back with her older sister, Joanna. She was telling her all about Frankie who was a new boy from America and how cool he was. That was when Tom found out how cold the railings were. He had slipped and leaned out to grab a hand-hold. But the park railings were so cold that his hand had stuck to them. It was like touching the lollies in the freezer.

Of course, he didn't say anything. Once his hand was free, he waited till they were all gathered round. 'Kiss the railings,' he said, looking straight at Kim, 'and I'll give you my 13-colour biro.' Kim had always wanted a decent biro. Without thinking, she leaned forwards and put her lips to the black railings.

As soon she touched the metal, she felt its icy bite and as she pulled away her lips stuck fast. She could feel the skin tearing. She stopped pulling and stayed still, bent double. The others were laughing, especially Tom.

'Someone's coming,' hissed Steve and with that they all cleared off, even Joanna. Kim kept gently tugging, trying to prise her lips off the railings. That was when she heard the footsteps approaching. Then she could see someone's trainers and trousers. Then the worst thing ever – someone spoke. And it was not just any old person; it was the new kid, Frankie. She did a cherry, and with a tug, pulled herself off the railings.

Politely, he handed her a clean tissue and she dabbed at her lips. Then they walked along Downsell Avenue towards school. He wanted to know what had happened and somehow Kim found that it was easy to talk to him. He told her all about coming from America and where he had lived in Chicago.

On the way, they passed a group of children. Tom had fallen over and was crying. Perhaps he shouldn't have been running along with the others, thought Kim. Silly to follow the crowd; why couldn't he think for himself?

# Fiction models

# Kissing the Railings

| | |
|---|---|
| **Opening to introduce main character** | Question opening to draw the reader in |

'Do you always do what your brothers tell you? Supposing they told you to jump off a bridge, I suppose you'd do that?' Kim had heard it often enough but it wasn't easy being the youngest of five. She was always the one to be caught, the one to fall over and hurt herself.

*Set up the main character*

That morning they had awoken to a world of white. The High Street traffic was at a standstill. The streets seemed eerily silent. Even the birds were not up to much. Sparrows hunched on telegraph wires, their feathers puffed up to keep them warm.

*Build the setting by description*

**Gradual build-up to the main event**

They left for school early, **straggling down the road, kicking at icy puddles, sliding on the pavement**. Kim kept to the back with her older sister, Joanna. She was telling her all about Frankie who was a new boy from America and how cool he was. That was when Tom found out how cold the railings were. He had slipped and leaned out to grab a hand-hold. But the park railings were so cold that his hand had stuck to them. It was like touching the lollies in the freezer.

*Add on '-ing' clauses for events*

*Use the occasional simile*

**Introduce dilemma – the main event**

Of course, he didn't say anything. Once his hand was free, he waited till they were all gathered round. 'Kiss the railings,' he said, looking straight at Kim, 'and I'll give you my 13-colour biro.' Kim had always wanted a decent biro. **Without thinking,** she leaned forwards and put her lips to the black railings.

*Use connectives to vary sentence openings*

*Show a character's thoughts (or lack of them!)*

**Dwelling on the dilemma**

**As** soon she touched the metal, she felt its icy bite and as she pulled away her lips stuck fast. She could feel the skin tearing. She stopped pulling and **stayed still,** bent double. The others were laughing, especially Tom.

*Occasional alliteration*

**Resolution**

'Someone's coming,' hissed Steve and with that they all cleared off, even Joanna. Kim kept gently tugging, trying to prise her lips off the railings. That was when she heard the footsteps approaching. **Then** she could see someone's trainers and trousers. **Then** the worst thing ever – someone spoke. And it was not just any old person; it was the new kid, Frankie. She did a cherry, and with a tug, pulled herself off the railings.

*Deliberate repetition to build up the events*

Adverb starter

**Politely,** he handed her a clean tissue and she dabbed at her lips. Then they walked along Downsell Avenue towards school. **He wanted to know what had happened and somehow Kim found that it was easy to talk to him.** He told her all about coming from America and where he had lived in Chicago.

Reveal character's thoughts and feelings

Ending

On the way, they passed a group of children. Tom had fallen over and was crying. Perhaps he shouldn't have been running along with the others, thought Kim. **Silly to follow the crowd; why couldn't he think for himself?**

Return to the opening at the end

# The Growler

When I was seven years old, I moved up to the Juniors. That meant walking further down Silchester Avenue, past Mrs Winterberry's corner shop and onto the High Street. The Juniors was wedged between Carter's Wood yard and the new chippie, Sharky's.

That first day will stick in my mind for ever. Of course, I knew everyone but none of us knew our teacher. She was new to the school so we had not met her on our visit at the end of the summer term.

My Mum let me walk on my own with Petie. 'Now you're in the Juniors, I can trust you,' she said and then she bent down and gave me a kiss. Honestly, right in front of Petie.

We made a face at each other and set off. The café on the High Street had been open for a while and we hung around the door, sniffing the scent of fried breakfast and toast. I'd not eaten much that morning because I'd been half nervous and half excited.

Anyway, in the end we got to the school, pressed the buzzer and the door clicked open. The playground seemed to be shimmering with noise and children. Petie and I just stood and stared. Then we started recognising kids from previous years – and some who were in our class.

We hung about in a corner near some dustbins and kicked at stones. A few others joined us till the whistle went. The whole playground stopped still, frozen like statues. Everyone that is, except for Cobber. But then he always was the last to cotton on. He was roaring round with his arms spread out, pretending to be an aeroplane zooming in for attack.

'Will the Mig Fighter in blue shorts STAND STILL,' bellowed the teacher. Cobber slowed down and then stopped. He stood with a silly grin looking at the teacher. It was a man teacher.

'That's Gatenby,' whispered Petie. He knew all the teachers' names because his sister was in the Upper Juniors. We waited till the second blast and all the other kids ran into lines. The rest of us didn't know where to go, till Mr Gatenby shouted again and pointed to where we should form a line. Then all the teachers started coming out to fetch their classes. The second one out was a huge woman dressed in what looked like a large sack. She wobbled as she walked, her pink cheeks jumping up and down. Petie and I shared a look, then a sigh of relief as she made her way towards an older class.

Then our teacher appeared and we all stared hard. She was beautiful. Even though I was only a kid back then, I could see it. She had amazing golden hair dangling down in ringlets, and huge blue eyes. She was called Miss Willet and yes, we would behave ourselves.

We filed in, hung up our bags and sat down in the classroom. It was love at first sight. I just couldn't take my eyes off her. I was mesmerised. Her voice was soft and smooth. I could have listened for ever.

'Now, let's start the day with a song,' she said, as she settled down at the piano. The class crowded round in an unruly bunch beside the piano and Miss Willet began to play.

I could see her glancing in my direction and it looked as if she was listening hard. So I smiled back and sang even louder, my heart thumping madly.

Suddenly, she stopped. 'Somebody is making a terrible growling noise. Who is it?' No one replied. I stared round at the rest of class, wondering who could have been so shameful as to ruin the song. When I looked back at Miss Willet, she was staring straight at me. 'It's you,' she said. 'Don't sing any more. You're spoiling it. Just open and close your mouth.'

So, that is how it happened. At that moment, I learned that my voice was only good for growling. Blinking back the tears, I opened and closed my mouth like a goldfish out of water.

# Top Cat

That morning we awoke to snow. It stretched for miles, in a wash of white. Tom and I crowded the windowsill and stared out.

Half an hour later, we were trudging up the lane to get a loaf of bread from the corner shop. We left the road and took the lagger that snaked up between the houses on the hill. Every now and then we stopped to catch our breath. It was so cold that the hand railing was covered in a thin layer of ice. Our boots crunched as we walked.

The shop was warm and my cheeks tingled. Clutching the loaf of bread, we wound our way back down, careful not to slip. Just by Codger's barn we heard the sound of a cat. A soft meow that seemed louder in the silence of the snow. For some reason, we both stopped and looked at each other.

A moment later, we had scrambled over the wall and were searching along the length of the barn, peering in through the wooden slats. The door was just ajar, so we slipped in. Our eyes adjusted to the dark and the stacks of straw bales came into view.

I scrambled up to the top, led by the plaintive crying of the cat. Tom stood by the door on guard. We had crossed old Codger more than once by mucking about on his land and he had never heard of the Geneva Convention, let alone the RSPCC. Only a week before we had felt the bite of his tongue. It wouldn't be past him to give us a clout, whatever the government said!

# Fiction models

**TERM 2: NARRATIVE: FINDING STORY (REFLECTION BACK IN TIME)**
(Easier)

Then I found them. Two kittens. One was white, quite still, and obviously dead. The other was tiny and so thin that I could feel its ribs. Its little mouth opening and shutting, as it called. I guessed the mother had not fed it in a while and now the kitten was desperate.

Picking it up, I tucked it under my coat. A minute later, we were making our way back down the lagger as fast as we could, skidding and whooping, down to the lane. I nursed the tiny bundle all the way home.

Mum found us an old pipette and drop-by-drop we fed the kitten warm milk. It was black and white and no bigger than my hand. My Mum reckoned that its mother might have been killed by the cold and if we hadn't rescued it, then it too would have died. I called it 'Top Cat' and it slept in a box in the airing cupboard where it was warm.

That was the winter I found my first real pet. Maybe it doesn't sound much but even now I think back to those few frail cries that echoed out across the snow. And I wonder, what would have happened if we had ignored them and hurried back to the warmth of our home?

## TERM 2: **NARRATIVE: FINDING STORY (REFLECTION BACK IN TIME)**
### (Easier)

# Top Cat

Short sentences can make punchy openings

Short paragraphs are better than very long ones!

**That morning we awoke to snow.** It stretched for miles, in a wash of white. Tom and I crowded the windowsill and stared out.

Opening that sets the scene

**Half an hour later,** we were trudging up the lane to get a loaf of bread from the corner shop. We left the road and took the **lagger**\* that snaked up between the houses on the hill. Every now and then we stopped to catch our breath. It was so cold that the hand railing was covered in a thin layer of ice. **Our boots crunched as we walked.**

Use time connectives to move action forwards

Short sentences give impact

The shop was warm and my cheeks tingled. **Clutching the loaf of bread,** we wound our way back down, careful not to slip. Just by Codger's barn we heard the sound of a cat. A **soft meow** that seemed louder in the silence of the snow. For some reason, we both stopped and looked at each other.

Use '-ing' clauses to start sentences

Mention sounds

Build-up of events that leads main character towards dilemma

A moment later, we had **scrambled** over the wall and were searching along the length of the barn, peering in through the wooden slats. The door was just ajar, so we slipped in. Our eyes adjusted to the dark and the stacks of straw bales came into view.

Use powerful verbs to suggest how characters feel

I scrambled up to the top, **led by the plaintive crying of the cat**. Tom stood by the door on guard. We had crossed old Codger more than once by mucking about on his land and he had never heard of the Geneva Convention, let alone the RSPCC. **Only a week before** we had felt the bite of his tongue. It wouldn't be past him to give us a clout, whatever the government said!

Tag on extra '-ing' clauses to build action

Brief flashback to a previous event

Give background to important characters

Short sentence for drama

Sentence fragment

Dilemma – the key event

**Then I found them. Two kittens.** One was white, quite still, and obviously dead. The other was tiny and so thin that I could feel its ribs. Its little mouth opening and shutting, as it called. I guessed the mother had not fed it in a while and now the kitten was desperate.

\*lagger = alleyway

## TERM 2: **NARRATIVE: FINDING STORY (REFLECTION BACK IN TIME)**
(Easier)

'-ing' starter for variety

Time connective to move action forwards

**Picking it up,** I tucked it under my coat. **A minute later,** we were making our way back down the lagger as fast as we could, skidding and whooping, down to the lane. I nursed the tiny bundle all the way home.

Resolution – sorting out dilemma

Mum found us an old pipette and drop-by-drop we fed the kitten warm milk. It was black and white and no bigger than my hand. My Mum reckoned that its mother might have been killed by the cold and if we hadn't rescued it, then it too would have died. I called it 'Top Cat' and it slept in a box in the airing cupboard where it was warm.

Homely description of events

Ending – reflecting back on importance of events

That was the winter I found my first real pet. Maybe it doesn't sound much but even now I think back to those **few frail cries that echoed out across the snow.** And I wonder, what would have happened if we had ignored them and hurried back to the warmth of our home?

Use of repeated sounds to make this memorable

Question at end to make reader wonder

# Sam's Thief

Sam woke with a start. He lay in the darkness and listened. What had woken him? His first thought took him straight back to the night that the car had been stolen. They're at it again, he muttered to himself.

Hardly breathing, he lay still and listened. At first he could hear nothing – just the distant sound of the cars on the Cirencester road, the wind tugging at the trees and the central heating gurgling.

Then he heard it. Something was moving about, outside in the garden. He definitely could hear the sound of someone moving through the bushes, pausing and then moving on, almost carelessly as if the noise didn't matter.

Probably some drunk from the pub, thought Sam. He was just about to roll over and go back to sleep when it hit him. It had only been a few weeks back that he had woken to find the car's aerial snapped! Perhaps it was the same person . . . silently, Sam slid out of bed, not wanting to disturb anyone else.

Cautiously, he crept down the stairs, one at a time, skipping the fourth, which he knew would creak. At the bottom he paused, and calmed his breathing. Tugging the front door open, he peered out into the darkness.

From the end of the garden, he could hear the sound of someone moving around. Someone – or something. Sam paused and wondered whether he should wake the others. Scaring kids off was one thing, but tackling a drunken burglar might be dangerous. For a moment he

TERM 2: **NARRATIVE: FINDING STORY (REFLECTION BACK IN TIME)**
(Harder)

wondered what on earth would happen if the other person had a gun. He saw himself, reeling back from the blast . . .

But what happened next was quite unexpected. He heard a loud crunch. It was rather like someone chewing on a boiled sweet. Silently, Sam crouched low. He tiptoed down the side of the house towards the bottom of the garden, towards the noise.

As he came to the end of the house, he stopped. At that moment, the clouds slipped away from the moon and he could see the garden quite clearly, a still and silent picture held in a silvery light. There, by the wall at the end of the garden, was the intruder, staring back at him. Not a person eating boiled sweets. No.

It was a badger, crunching snails.

# The Sack

Once upon a time Mullah Nasrudin was walking from one place to another when he met a man going in the other direction. This poor fellow was frowning and had his head down.

'What on earth is the matter, old friend?' asked Mullah kindly. Immediately, the man stopped and began to pour out his woes. It was a long tale and the sun was hot but Mullah waited patiently as the man told him how he had lost his job, been thrown from his house and his wife had left him! Why, even his family and friends had cast him aside. So he had taken to a life on the road but even there he had been dogged by ill luck. He had slept in a ditch and had been robbed of the shirt from his back.

'Never,' he sniffed, 'has a man been so unlucky.' Saying this, he held up his tattered old bag and said, 'Why, all I have got left in the world is inside this bag.'

'Why that's terrible,' said Mullah, seizing the bag and dashing off down the road.

The poor man burst into tears, for now he had lost everything save his poor, weak body and his soul. Wearily he walked on, hardly able to put one foot in front of the other. And all the while he wondered what he had done to deserve so much ill luck.

Meanwhile, Mullah had run round the corner and placed the man's bag right in the middle of the road. Having done that, he hid in the trees at the side of the road and waited to see what would happen. He did not have to wait for long.

## TERM 3: **NARRATIVE: TRADITIONAL TALE (THREE SUFI STORIES)**
(Easier)

A few minutes later, the poor man stumbled round the corner, tears streaming down his face. As soon as he saw his bag, he stopped and cried out, 'My bag, my dear old bag. I thought I had lost you.'
He sprinted forwards and seized the bag, his face beaming with smiles.

Mullah sat back and grinned to himself. He liked to spread a little joy.

     *       *       *

Nasrudin was on his way home with some fresh goat's meat. He had just borrowed a recipe from a friend and was going to make a pie. Unfortunately, a buzzard swooped down, seized the meat and flew off.

'Fool!' shouted Nasrudin, 'I've still got the recipe!'

     *       *       *

The Hoja was busy throwing cake crumbs round his house.

'What are you doing that for?' asked a neighbour.

'It scares off lions.'

'But there are no lions in this area.'

'So, there you are – it works,' replied the Hoja.

## TERM 3: **NARRATIVE: TRADITIONAL TALE (THREE SUFI STORIES)**
### (Easier)

# The Sack

| | |
|---|---|
| **Opening introduces two main characters** | Once upon a time Mullah Nasrudin was walking from one place to another when he met a man going in the other direction. This **poor** fellow was **frowning** and **had his head down**. |

*Quickly establishing how character feels*

| | |
|---|---|
| **Build-up – the background information** | 'What on earth is the matter, old friend?' asked Mullah kindly. Immediately, the man stopped and began to pour out his woes. It was a long tale and the sun was hot but Mullah waited patiently as the man told him how he had lost his job, been thrown from his house and his wife had left him! Why, even his family and friends had cast him aside. So he had taken to a life on the road but even there he had been dogged by ill luck. He had slept in a ditch and had been robbed of the shirt from his back. |

*A catalogue of disasters!*

'Never,' he sniffed, 'has a man been so unlucky.' Saying this, he held up his tattered old bag and said, 'Why, all I have got left in the world is inside this bag.'

*Short paragraphs are OK*

| | |
|---|---|
| **Dilemma** | 'Why that's terrible,' said Mullah, seizing the bag and dashing off down the road. |

The poor man burst into tears, for now he had lost everything save his poor, weak body and his soul. Wearily he walked on, hardly able to put one foot in front of the other. And all the while he wondered what he had done to deserve so much ill luck.

*Show how a character feels by their actions and revealing their thoughts*

| | |
|---|---|
| **Useful connective for shifting events** | **Meanwhile**, Mullah had run round the corner and placed the man's bag right in the middle of the road. **Having done that**, he hid in the trees at the side of the road and waited to see what would happen. He did not have to wait for long. |

*'-ing' starter to vary sentence openings*

**Resolution**

| | |
|---|---|
| **Useful time connectives to move story forward** | **A few minutes later**, the poor man stumbled round the corner, tears streaming down his face. **As soon as** he saw his bag, he stopped and cried out, 'My bag, my dear old bag. I thought I had lost you.' He sprinted forwards and seized the bag, **his face beaming with smiles**. |

*Tag on a clause*

| | |
|---|---|
| **Joke ending** | Mullah sat back and grinned to himself. He liked to spread a little joy. |

\*            \*            \*

## TERM 3: **NARRATIVE: TRADITIONAL TALE (THREE SUFI STORIES)**
(Easier)

Nasrudin was on his way home with some fresh goat's meat. He had just borrowed a recipe from a friend and was going to make a pie. Unfortunately, a buzzard swooped down, seized the meat and flew off.

'Fool!' shouted Nasrudin, 'I've still got the recipe!'

\*　　　\*　 .　 　\*

Two short tales that could be used for elaboration

The Hoja was busy throwing cake crumbs round his house.

'What are you doing that for?' asked a neighbour.

'It scares off lions.'

'But there are no lions in this area.'

'So, there you are – it works,' replied the Hoja.

# The King and the Fisher Boy

Once upon a time there was a King and Queen who lived on the edge of a deep, dark forest. They had one child – a little girl who was their most precious treasure.

Just after she had been born, the King held a great party to celebrate her birth. He invited all the wise women to give their presents but forgot to invite one old hen wife who lived in the forest. Just as the feast had started, the hen wife strode into the party. She was furious that she had not been invited.

'Your daughter will marry a boy who was born on the same day, at the same hour, under the same star. And that boy will be so poor that he will not even have two pennies to rub together,' she muttered, over the baby's cradle.

The King was worried because he knew that whatever the hen wife said was bound to come true. So he sent out his soldiers to the far corners of his land to try and find a baby that had been born on the same day, at the same hour, under the same star. But one by one they returned, having found nothing.

In the end, the King decided that he would have to search himself. So he put aside his rich clothes and dressed up in the rough clothes of a beggar. All he took with him was a small purse of gold and his signet ring but these he kept well hidden.

He travelled to the far corners of his kingdom, searching for the child born under the same star as his daughter. He crossed the great river where the icy water flowed down from the mountains and the great brown bears waited to scoop out the salmon. He stood on top of the tallest mountain and stared at the eagles as they wheeled in the sky. He stalked through the deep forests and listened to the creatures that lived in darkness and the wind whispering through the leaves. He sat at the crossroads, not knowing whether luck lay to the left or right or straight ahead.

One day he came to a little mill by a small stream. The old mill wheel was turning and the miller was hard at work. The King fell into conversation with the miller who invited him to sup with him and his wife and to stay the night. After they had eaten a meal of simple soup and bread, they sat by the fire and smoked a pipe. The King was staring at the flames dancing when he heard the sound of a baby crying.

# Fiction models

'Why, that is my son,' said the miller, shaking his head. 'I love him dearly but we are so poor that we hardly have two pennies to rub together . . .' Casually, the King asked when the lad had been born, and sure enough, he had been born under the same star as his own daughter, the princess.

The King now knew that his search was at an end. He told the miller that he was the King and that he wanted to give the miller something in return for his hospitality. At first the miller did not believe the King until the King showed the miller the purse of gold and his signet ring. The King offered to take in the boy and bring him up in the palace as if he were his own.

'Think of it, when the north wind brings snow, he will be warm; when the days are lean, his belly will be full; why, he will even be taught how to read and write; how to ride a horse and fight.'

Early the next morning, the miller and his poor wife decided that it was best for their son and so they put him in a small wooden box, wrapped him in a thin cotton blanket and gave him to the King.

The King said goodbye, his talk full of promises and his heart heavy with what he had to do. He walked down the stream till it came to the sea. There he walked along the sands and out into waves, holding the box high above his head. And when he was so far out that the waves lapped at his chin, he set the box on the water and pushed. For he had not the heart to kill the child outright. And that was the thanks that he gave to the miller for his kindness . . .

Then the King began his journey home.

Now at that time there lived down by the sea a fisherman and he was sitting on the rocks mending his nets when he heard his dog barking. Now old Sam never barked for any foolish reason, so the fisherman left his nets to see what Sam had found. To his amazement, he saw a small wooden box on the shoreline. And from the box came a whimpering sound.

Now the baby was like a blessing to the fisherman because he and his wife had not been able to have any children, and many days they had prayed and it seemed to him as if at last their prayers had been answered. He stood on the beach and held the baby high above his head and called out his thanks. Then he took the baby home.

Now it was 18 years later that the King set out hunting because there was a rumour that a white stag had been seen in the forest. After two days, a shout went up and the King and his men were galloping through the trees, chasing the white stag. But it always seemed to be too far ahead for an arrow and the chase took them mile after mile deep into a part of the forest where they had never been before. In the end the King left his men behind, for he had to catch the stag for himself. What he did not know was that the forest ended just ahead, right on the edge of a cliff!

He galloped on as fast as his horse would take him, with the white stag just ahead when suddenly they broke free of the trees and the stag leapt into the air over the cliff's edge. The King tugged on his reins and his horse managed to stop just in time but the King was flung over the edge . . .

Down on the sands was a young fisher boy, mending his father's nets. He saw the King fall and land on the cliffside, snared by a bush. So, taking a rope, the boy climbed the cliff's edge where the gulls wheeled. He tied the rope round the King and brought him down onto the sands. The King had broken his leg so the boy fetched his pony and trap. A while later the King was in the fisherman's cottage, resting in bed.

All that week the family cared for the King, as if he were their own. 'Why, he's a fine lad, your son,' said the King to the fisherman.

'Well, he is to be sure . . . but he isn't really mine,' replied the fisherman. And he settled down to tell the King the tale of how he found the boy in an old wooden box, wrapped in a thin cotton blanket. The King realised that this had to be the boy who was born under the same star as his daughter, and his pride and fear flared. So, thinking fast, he asked the fisherman if his son would take a letter back to the palace, asking for his men to bring a wagon to take him home. But in the letter he wrote an order for the boy to be killed.

Now the fisher boy set off through the forest, carrying the King's letter. Mile after mile he walked until night began to fall and he could no longer find his way. Just as he thought that he might have to sleep outside, he noticed a cottage. The old lady there let him in and soon the exhausted boy was fast asleep. But later that night, the robbers who lived there returned. They stole the letter from the boy's knapsack and read the contents. Now the King's men had been chasing them so they had no love for him. So, the old lady, who was the leader of the gang of thieves, took the letter and changed its contents, instructing the Queen that the boy should marry the princess right away.

The next day the boy set off, and sooner rather than later he reached the castle with the letter. The Queen liked the boy immediately and so too did the princess. They obeyed the letter and made ready for the wedding feast while a wagon was sent back for the King.

Well, the fisher boy and the princess were married. The sun shone, the brides-maids threw apple blossom of pink and white over the couple and the feast began with much singing and laughter.

Once everyone had finished eating, a storyteller stepped forwards and began to tell the tale of a hunter who caught a wren. But the wren pleaded for its life. 'Save me, I'm not worth eating and besides – if you do, I'll tell you three truths.' So the hunter set the wren free and it flew to the top of the nearest tree where it perched. 'The first truth is that you should never listen to the stories of a liar.' The hunter nodded, for this was good advice. 'You should have killed me,' continued the sparrow, 'for yesterday, I flew down to the princess's chamber and there I swallowed a ruby as red as fire and as large as an apple.' At this, the hunter began to rant and rave.

'You're right, I should have killed you,' he said, raising his bow to shoot.

But the wren flew higher, calling, 'Why, already you have forgotten my first truth – I'm so small that I could never have swallowed a gem as large as an apple. My third truth is this – a fool's trap will often be emptied, for he is too easily tempted!'

As the storyteller moved on to tell more tales, the King's wagon returned. The Queen, the princess and the fisher boy ran to greet him. From the crowd, an old hen wife watched the King's face as he saw the fisher boy and heard the Queen tell him how pleased they had been to receive his letter telling them to arrange such a wedding feast ... And from the crowd, the old hen wife smiled to herself at the King's muted rage. For he knew that he had been tricked and there was nothing that he could do. Her words had been true and had now become life.

# Jack O'Lantern

Last night, I slept in a wren's nest. The darkness dragged a film of frost across the leaves. I pulled my sheep-fur cloak over my head and tried to think warm dreams.

I woke at dawn, just as the sun crept over the fields. In the orange light, I heard them coming. A distant grumbling at first and then the ground thudding and the oak tree shaking as they strode by. There were two of them, both taller than the tree.

I took a drink of dew from an acorn's cup and flew down to the brambles. A lazy tortoiseshell fluttered weakly by, sipping at the old berries. I found one hidden under the leaves, soft and sweet. It stained my hands dark purple.

As the day warmed up, I snoozed in a foxglove. The sun filtered through the petals in a soft purple. It was then that I smelled the strong, stale sweat and felt the sudden shudder of the ground. Stealthily, it had crept up on me. I saw its red eye staring in. Tighter than a woodlouse, I curled into a ball. But it had me, tipped me out and rolled me onto the rough skin of its hand.

It popped me into a jar like a fly. Placing the jar in its stinking pocket, it thudded off, bouncing me round like a pea in a pod. The sides of the jar were smooth and I slid about, staring out at the dark folds of its tunic.

The next thing I knew, I was out in bright light, lying stunned at the bottom of the jar. There were more of them gathered round. They held me up to the light and peered in, their great red eyes like angry suns staring at me.

I could hear them discussing whether I was worth eating. Luckily, it was considered that I was too small and not worth the effort. The one that had caught me wondered if I had a sting. I sat in the glass and scowled, trying to look as fierce as possible. But I kept my wings curled tight. Never show your wings, my Ma had warned me.

In the end, they tired of me and wandered off. Their footsteps echoed, sending tremors through the jar. After a while there was silence. Only the sound of a fly cruising the floor for crumbs.

I waited a while, cautious as a hedge mouse. Then I uncurled my wings, and fluttered up and out of the jar. I flew straight through the open window and back to the nettle patch where Ma gave me the scolding of my life.

I slept all afternoon, dreaming of Ogres.

# Fiction models

## Jack O'Lantern

| Annotation | Text | Annotation |
|---|---|---|

**Surprise opening to make reader wonder who or what is the main character**

**Opening introduces main character**

Last night, **I slept in a wren's nest.** The **darkness dragged** a **film of frost** across the leaves. I pulled my sheep-fur cloak over my head and tried to think warm dreams.

*Alliteration makes phrases memorable*

**Build-up – foreshadows dilemma**

I woke at dawn, just as the sun crept over the fields. In the orange light, I heard them coming. A distant grumbling at first and then the ground thudding and the oak tree shaking as they strode by. There were two of them, both taller than the tree.

*Building the picture of another world – like ours but with a few differences*

**Invented detail**

**Lulls reader into a false sense of security**

I took a drink of **dew** from an **acorn's cup** and flew down to the brambles. A lazy tortoiseshell fluttered weakly by, sipping at the old berries. I found one hidden under the leaves, soft and sweet. It stained my hands dark purple.

*Use what you know and invent a bit*

As the day warmed up, I snoozed in a foxglove. The sun filtered through the petals in a soft purple. It was then that I smelled the strong, stale sweat and felt the sudden shudder of the ground.

*Use description to build image*

**Adverb opener**

**Dilemma – main event**

**Stealthily**, it had crept up on me. I saw its red eye staring in. Tighter than a woodlouse, I curled into a ball. But it had me, tipped me out and rolled me onto the rough skin of its hand.

It popped me into a jar like a fly. **Placing the jar in its stinking pocket,** it thudded off, bouncing me round like a pea in a pod. The sides of the jar were smooth and I slid about, **staring out at the dark folds of its tunic.**

*'-ing' starter*

*Add on an '-ing' clause*

The next thing I knew, I was out in bright light, lying **stunned** at the bottom of the jar. There were more of them gathered round. They held me up to the light and peered in, their great red eyes **like angry suns** staring at me.

*Use powerful verbs*

*Use similes*

**Next events – as a result of dilemma**

I could hear them discussing whether I was worth eating. **Luckily**, it was considered that I was too small and not worth the effort. The one that had caught me wondered if I had a sting. I sat in the glass and scowled, trying to look as fierce as possible. **But** I kept my wings curled tight. Never show your wings, my Ma had warned me.

*Adverb opener*

*Use 'But' at start of a sentence for emphasis*

# Fiction models

TERM 3: **NARRATIVE: FANTASY**
(Easier)

Useful connective to move action towards end

Use the senses

Invented fantasy simile!

Only reveal a clue at the end!

Resolution

Ending

**In the end,** they tired of me and wandered off. Their footsteps echoed, sending tremors through the jar. After a while there was silence. Only the sound of a fly cruising the floor for crumbs.

I waited a while, **cautious as a hedge mouse.** Then I uncurled my wings, and fluttered up and out of the jar. I flew straight through the open window and back to the nettle patch where Ma gave me the scolding of my life.

I slept all afternoon, dreaming of Ogres.

# Thog's Journey

Two hundred and thirty years is young for a dwarf but Thog felt old in his bones. It had been a long climb up the mountain and at last he had reached the summit. It's not far to Harmsway Forest, they had told him. Not far! It was at least 12 leagues.

Thog, so named because he had been born in a mist but his mother could not spell, sat by the cairn at the top of the ridge and stared down the slope towards the distant forest. Somewhere in there was his destination, the stone tower. Word had reached the dwarves that their old friend, the beekeeper Olafson, was sick and needed the root of hemp's foot.

Thog had drawn the shortest straw and so it was he who had been sent. He had tried to get out of it by hiding in a storm drain but it was no use. Old goody Mina had sniffed him out with her long, warty nose. Unceremoniously, he'd been dragged out by his hair and brought before the counsel. Trying to hide had sealed his fate.

Dwarves should be underground digging, he thought to himself as the sun set in a scarlet haze beyond the forest, making it look as if it was on fire. A short way down, he found a small cave and snuggled into his fur-lined cape for the night. He had learned a trick or two several years earlier in the mines of Moravia and knew a little bit about shape shifting. Anyone glancing in would have seen a large stone rather than a sleeping dwarf. It was a useful trick and would mean an undisturbed night of sleep.

First thing the next morning, Thog woke as daylight slipped in through the cave mouth. He sat in the entrance, looking down onto the forest. Quietly, he smoked his pipe. He could just see the tip of the tower poking above the trees. It was not too far from the forest's edge and should be easy enough to find.

As he sat there, he began to have the most uncomfortable feeling that he was being watched. Quickly, but without rushing, he packed his knapsack and began to trudge down.

A moment later, there came a scuffle of stones behind him and a sharp yelp. Thog glanced over his shoulder and saw a pair of grey mountain wolves bounding from rock to rock down towards him. It was obvious that they were not out to offer some sort of welcome. He could see their ribs sticking out! Almost without thinking, Thog turned himself into a stone. The wolves must have been amazed to see their breakfast disappear and a large boulder roll on down the mountain at great speed.

The bottom came with a terrible thump. Luckily, Thog had been padded against the wintry weather. Checking his arms and legs, he sat there for a while letting his breath return. High above him, he heard a long, plaintive howl echoing. Thog grinned to himself. He hadn't fancied being a wolf's breakfast.

Half a day's travel later, Thog reached the edge of the forest. He stood looking up at the great trees. They seemed very tall to one so small. And what was more, they were close together. So close, in fact, that there seemed little room for daylight. As he stepped into the trees, the light diminished and so too did all the sounds. It was eerily quiet and all that he could hear was the crackle of dried twigs and leaves underfoot. He marched on in a straight line, taking the direction of the stone tower, peering anxiously between the trees.

A short while later, he saw that he was about to step into a clearing and in the clearing was the tall, stone tower of the beekeeper. Thog had always been a cautious dwarf and so he hid behind a tree. He was waiting to see if the coast was clear.

It was quite quiet except for a few chickens, scratching about the base of the tower. There was a pile of logs with a long, rusty saw and a sharpened axe beside it. On the other side of the clearing stood a row of white, wooden hives. He could hear the restless buzz of the bees.

At that moment, the tower door swung open and out strode the beekeeper. He was at least sixteen hands tall and burly as a black bear. Ambling down to the hives, he began fussing. Bees swarmed round him but he did not seem to care. Thog imagined that Olafson was singing to them.

Then the beekeeper straightened up, turned and called. 'Come on out, my friend. I know you're there. My bees are my eyes and ears.' Thog made his way across the clearing and shook Olafson's mighty paw. Once he was close, he could see that the beekeeper really was blind.

Feeling slightly nervous, Thog handed over the small parcel of herbs. He had never met anyone so huge before. So that is what a giant looks like, he thought to himself. Olafson sniffed the herbs, nodded his head and then he turned to pick up a large stone jar of honey. Silently and graciously, he handed it to Thog in exchange.

Obviously a man of few words, thought Thog. Probably comes of living out here on his own. Shouldering the jar, Thog stammered his thanks. The beekeeper stooped, shook the dwarf's hand and gently shook his head. A tiny bee rose up from Olafson's hair. It was a brilliant gold and shimmered as it flew onto the dwarf's shoulder. It settled there, closed its wings and seemed to freeze, till it looked more like an elaborate brooch than any living thing.

Thog knew that the bee must be some sort of lucky charm. He watched the beekeeper wend his way back to the stone tower, turned and began the long journey home, laden down with the finest clover honey.

All he had to do now was climb back up and nip past the wolves. Sooner rather than later, he would be back in his own home. But that is another story and what happened to Thog on his return journey will have to wait for another day of telling. But before this tale is spent, one word of warning. Thog would tell you himself – never kill a bee, for it is not only honey that they make . . .

## TERM 3: **NARRATIVE: MODEL PLAN FOR EXTENDED FANTASY QUEST**
(Easier)

**Main character:**   Thog the Dwarf.
Small and sturdy.
Brave – and cunning – can shape-shift.

**Companions:**   Helen – a serving girl from the castle.
Really is a princess but doesn't know it.
Thinks she is an orphan.
Small and brave.

**Where do they start their journey:** From the king's castle.
Thog is sent by king.
Helen is running away.

**Where are they going:** To find the wizard, Zander.
Lives in lonely tower.
Old and wise.

**Why are they going there (task):** To ask him for a potion to
cure the old king's unsteady heart.
King very ill – finding it hard to rule.

**Three main places they journey through:**
a.  Misty mountains – dark and treacherous; snow-bound; mountain
wolves live there – caves can be used for shelter.
b.  Dark forest – huge trees; no light; trees can come alive; elves live there.
c.  Icy lake – frozen over; giant fish live underneath; can be walked upon;
they skate across.

**What they meet on the way:** Misty mountains – mountain wolves.
Dark forest – evil goblins!
Icy lake – sea serpent breaks ice.

## TERM 3: **NARRATIVE: MODEL PLAN FOR EXTENDED FANTASY QUEST**
(Easier)

**Main character:** Thog the Dwarf.

Small and sturdy.

Brave – and cunning – can **shape-shift.**

> Name

> A few details

> One special attribute

**Companions:** Helen – a serving girl from the castle.

Really is a princess but doesn't know it.

Thinks she is an orphan.

Small and brave.

> Work in note form or sketch quickly

**Where do they start their journey:** From the king's castle.

Thog is sent by king.

Helen is running away.

> Reasons for journey

**Where are they going:** To find the wizard, Zander.

Lives in lonely tower.

Old and wise.

**Why are they going there (task):** To ask him for a potion to

cure the old king's unsteady heart.

King very ill – finding it hard to rule.

> Task is usually to find or take something or someone somewhere

**Three main places they journey through:**

a. Misty mountains – dark and treacherous; snow-bound; mountain wolves live there – caves can be used for shelter.

b. Dark forest – huge trees; no light; trees can come alive; elves live there.

c. Icy lake – frozen over; giant fish live underneath; can be walked upon; they skate across.

> Decide on a few places

**What they meet on the way:** Misty mountains – mountain wolves.

Dark forest – evil goblins!

Icy lake – sea serpent breaks ice.

> Note down possible dilemmas for each setting

## TERM 3: **NARRATIVE: TEMPLATE OF PLAN FOR EXTENDED FANTASY QUEST**

Main character:

Companions:

Where do they start their journey:

Where are they going:

Why are they going there (task):

Three main places they journey through:

What they meet/happens on the way:

# Non-fiction models

## Police Report: Recent Wolf Attacks

In the last week there have been several attacks by a lone wolf on houses belonging to two pigs, who are both new to the area.

Mr Bacon only recently left home and travelled to this locality. He built his house from straw, as he was interested in conserving local materials and living in an environmentally friendly building. However, late on Thursday evening, a wolf tried to break in.

Mr Bacon reported: 'I was in the kitchen boiling up a soup when I heard a knock at the door. The wolf tried to persuade me to let him in. I asked him for identification and all that he could do was to threaten to blow the house down. I ignored him and carried on making the soup. A moment later, there was an almighty blast! I thought that there had been an earthquake. The walls tumbled down and I saw the wolf rushing towards the house. I scampered as quick as my trotters would carry me!'

The wolf in question was interviewed the following evening when he had been arrested lurking in the vicinity of an old lady's cottage. He is a grey wolf of medium build with no distinguishing marks. He looks undernourished and his ribs are showing. He claims that he has had former employment as an ice cream seller. However, he has no papers on him. He likes to talk a lot and it was difficult to stop him. He feels that the locals have picked on him.

## TERM 1: **BIOGRAPHICAL AND AUTOBIOGRAPHICAL WRITING**
### (Easier)

# Police Report: Recent Wolf Attacks

| Use of time connectives |

Orientation

**In the last week** there have been several attacks by a lone wolf on houses belonging to two pigs, who are both new to the area.

| Past tense, because events have already happened |

Background information to the incident

Mr Bacon only recently **left** home and **travelled** to this locality. He **built** his house from straw, as he was interested in **conserving local materials** and living in an environmentally friendly building. However, **late on** Thursday evening, a wolf tried to break in.

| Mix modern and traditional for humour |

| Time connective |

Use quotes

The pig's view

**Mr Bacon reported:** 'I was in the kitchen boiling up a soup when I heard a knock at the door. The wolf tried to persuade me to let him in. I asked him for identification and all that he could do was to threaten to blow the house down. I ignored him and carried on making the soup. A moment later, there was an almighty blast! I thought that there had been an earthquake. The walls tumbled down and I saw the wolf rushing towards the house. I scampered as quick as my trotters would carry me!'

| Prepare by hot-seating |

The wolf's view

The wolf in question was interviewed the following evening when he had been arrested lurking in the vicinity of an old lady's cottage. He is a grey wolf of medium build with no distinguishing marks. He looks undernourished and his ribs are showing. He claims that he has had former employment as an ice cream seller. However, he has no papers on him. He likes to talk a lot and it was difficult to stop him. He feels that the locals have picked on him.

| Basic description |

| Alternative view of the same incident |

# The Wolf's Autobiographical Account

I was born as one of 14 baby wolves into a large pack. However, I was the weakest of the pack and my parents never had much time for me. I did not do well at school and left as soon as I was able. My first winter I spent in the forest without any proper place to sleep. If I ever went anywhere near a village or farm, I was chased away. I tried selling icicles but there were not many takers! Many nights I spent shivering with the cold. In the end my asthma got so bad that I was huffing and puffing.

When spring came I saw some cottages being built in the area. I thought that I might be able to work for the builders and approached them. However, my cold got the better of me and I let out an almighty sneeze. Unfortunately, the house was very flimsy and only made of straw. Before I knew it, the straw house had been blown down and the owner was running away. I suppose he thought that I had done it on purpose. Immediately, I ran after the owner to reassure him that I would help him to rebuild his property but he only ran the faster.

When I saw that he had joined another builder who was putting up a house made of sticks, I approached with caution in case there were further misunderstandings. At that moment, I noticed a young girl dressed in red passing by. Her basket looked very heavy so I thought that I had better see if she wanted me to help. It was at that moment that I saw a woodcutter rushing after the girl. In fear for her life, I ran on and decided to lie in waiting in case the villain attacked her. Just after that, I was arrested.

# Catastrophes

Catastrophes are sudden disasters that are of unusual importance because of their size. Stepping on a cat's tail may be considered to be a catastrophe for the cat but in general terms would not be viewed as such by the majority of humans!

The sinking of the *Titanic* has been turned into a great film and is considered by many to be the worst catastrophe at sea. It is certainly the best known, probably because the ship's company had boasted that the *Titanic* was unsinkable. But it struck an iceberg and sank, drowning over 1,500 people. However, many people do not know of the far worse disaster when in 1945 a German ship was sunk by a submarine, drowning over 8,000 people, many of whom were children!

Volcanoes are always capable of producing a catastrophe. The worst incidence has to be when Krakatoa exploded. This event killed nearly 40,000 people! Not only did the explosion kill many people, but massive tidal waves also destroyed the coastline. Dust from the explosion was found across the world!

Many films have shown the sort of catastrophe that might occur if the earth was hit by a meteor. In the last hundred years two enormous meteors have struck the earth. Both could have destroyed a whole city if they had landed on one. However, a catastrophe was averted because they hit areas where there was no population. One landed in 1908 and the other in 1947 in Siberia. Not one person was hurt.

Catastrophes are feared by all of us. Luckily, they are few and far between. Most of us will never have to face a tidal wave, an exploding volcano or a meteorite landing in the back garden!

# Catastrophes

| Definition – explain the subject to the reader | Catastrophes **are** sudden disasters that are of unusual importance because of their size. Stepping on a cat's tail may be considered to be a catastrophe for the cat **but in general terms** would not be viewed as such by the majority of humans! | Present tense / Formality |

**The sinking of the *Titanic* has been turned into a great film and is considered by many to be the worst catastrophe at sea.** It is certainly the best known, probably because the ship's company had boasted that the *Titanic* was unsinkable. But it struck an iceberg and sank, drowning over 1,500 people. However, many people do not know of the far worse disaster when in 1945 a German ship was sunk by a submarine, drowning over 8,000 people, many of whom were children!

*Disasters at sea*

*Topic sentence introduces the subject matter of the paragraph*

*Use of specific facts and details*

**Volcanoes are always capable of producing a catastrophe.** The worst incidence has to be when Krakatoa exploded. This event killed nearly 40,000 people! Not only did the explosion kill many people, but massive tidal waves also destroyed the coastline. Dust from the explosion was found across the world!

*A volcanic catastrophe*

*Topic sentence*

*Try to include interesting facts*

**Many films have shown the sort of catastrophe that might occur if the earth was hit by a meteor.** In the last hundred years two enormous meteors have struck the earth. Both could have destroyed a whole city if they had landed on one. However, a catastrophe was averted because they hit areas where there was no population. One landed in 1908 and the other in 1947 in Siberia. **Not one person was hurt.**

*Meteoric catastrophe*

*Topic sentence*

*Short sentence for impact*

Catastrophes are **feared by all of us.** Luckily, they are few and far between. **Most of us will never have to face a tidal wave, an exploding volcano or a meteorite landing in the back garden!**

*Concluding points*

*Relate subject to the reader*

A touch of humour helps!

# Amazing Animals

Animals are amazing but most people only know about common pets such as cats and dogs. However, out in the wild some of the most extraordinary creatures live. Many have fascinating lives.

Vampire bats do exist and are not just found in films and the books of Darren Shan. However, the real creature is far removed from Dracula! They do not bite but scratch with their teeth until they draw blood. In fact, they are so gentle that you might not even wake up!

Goldfish have a memory that only lasts about seven seconds so that once it has been round the bowl, it may well have forgotten where it started! Rats have a memory that may only last about half a minute – maybe that's why they always look inquisitive because every half a minute everything is new all over again!

The black rhinoceros may well look like a fierce creature but it is the most gentle of souls really. Though it weighs in at over a ton, this gentle beast can be tamed. In fact, it will even eat from your hand!

Other odd facts:

• The Egyptians trained baboons to serve food;

• A hibernating woodchuck only breathes ten times an hour;

• Hippos give birth under water;

- Grizzly bears run as fast as a horse;

- In the fifteenth century packs of wolves roamed the streets of Paris.

If an alligator ever attacks you, this piece of information may come in handy. Though they have very powerful jaws that can break your bones with one mighty crunch, they have very weak muscles that open the jaws. This means that if an alligator attacks you, remember to hold its mouth shut. You should be able to accomplish this quite easily!

So, there you are – the amazing world of animals. Keep your eyes and ears open for other amazing facts about the extraordinary creatures that share this planet with us. Make sure that we preserve these creatures by not spoiling their habitats.

Piper's Cottage
Tale End
Goatshire

Dear Baron Hardup

I am writing to complain about the dreadful behaviour of your two stepdaughters, the Ugly Sisters, Ermintrude and Jezebel.

They have been making a nuisance of themselves while in the shopping centre. Only this morning I had to ask them to leave because they were throwing custard pies at the knave of tarts. They claimed that they had seen him stealing tarts from the bakery but there is no firm evidence to support their claim.

Furthermore, they come into town dressed in such a bright and vulgar fashion that they frighten the horses who are trying to mind their own business and pull carriages. Herds of cattle and sheep have been seen bolting in fear, as your stepdaughters look more like two mobile Christmas trees than human beings!

Finally, they have insulted the prince by pretending that they only take size six in shoes when anyone can see that their feet would need house-boats rather than anything too dainty.

I hope that you will be able to address these complaints.

Yours sincerely

The Mayor of Tale End

## TERM 1: **NON-FICTION REVISION: LETTERS**
### (Easier)

Piper's Cottage
Tale End
Goatshire

| Address |

Dear Baron Hardup

| Opening – introduces subject of letter |

| Formal tone |

**I am writing to complain** about the dreadful behaviour of your two step-daughters, the Ugly Sisters, Ermintrude and Jezebel.

| First complaint |

They have been making a nuisance of themselves while in the shopping centre. Only this morning I had to ask them to leave because they were throwing custard pies at the knave of tarts. They claimed that they had seen him stealing tarts from the bakery but **there is no firm evidence to support their claim.**

| Formal tone |

| Use connective to help 'add' more detail |

| Second complaint |

**Furthermore**, they come into town dressed in such a bright and vulgar fashion that they frighten the horses who are trying to mind their own business and pull carriages. Herds of cattle and sheep have been seen bolting in fear, as your stepdaughters look more like two mobile Christmas trees than human beings!

| Humour! |

| Third complaint |

Finally, they have insulted the prince by pretending that they only take size six in shoes when anyone can see that their feet would need house-boats rather than anything too dainty.

| End comment |

I hope that you will be able to address these complaints.

| Request that letter has led up to |

| Formal ending |

Yours sincerely

The Mayor of Tale End

Rookem
Grabbit Lane
Thiefshire

Dear Sir

I am writing to you on behalf of my client, Solomon Grundy. I note from my records that Mr Grundy was born on Monday to joyful parents. He was born a healthy boy, weighing as much as a fattened hen. On Tuesday, my records show that he was christened at the local church. The priest presiding over the matter was our local vicar, the Reverend Peter Piper. On Wednesday, the church records reveal that he was married to one Little Bo Peep whose bridesmaids were sheep. The matter of the mess that the sheep caused in the church was smoothed over as the vicar recognised that they had also trimmed the grass in the churchyard, which had got rather out of hand.

Although the marriage of Mr Grundy was a happy one, I was distressed to learn that he was taken ill on Thursday. His visit to the local doctors resulted in medicine being prescribed. I note that by Friday his conditioned had worsened.

However, his visit to your hospital on the evening of Friday should have meant that he would survive, but by Saturday morning he had died. I gather that my client's husband had been eating blackbird pie with the King and Queen and this may have poisoned him.

Do you have any evidence that he had been poisoned? If this is the case, I will have to take up the matter with His Majesty.

Yours sincerely

Mr Rookem, solicitor

# The Evacuation was Right

During the Second World War many children were evacuated to the countryside. This caused much controversy, but on reflection it was the right thing to do.

Long before war began, plans were drawn up to move children to the countryside because it was expected that the cities would be bombed.

Parents did not have to evacuate their children, though there was considerable pressure. It was considered to be dangerous for children to be in cities. The bombing would mean that their lives were at direct risk. Many also believed that the young should be sent away because they might prove to be a distraction from the daily war effort. It was also thought that it was important to preserve the next generation.

Of course, some parents could not bear the idea of being separated and others needed their children to help with their daily lives. It has to be remembered that some adults could not cope alone as they had been bombed out. In these cases, some children ended up fending for the family and themselves, little better than beggars on the street. This often led them into crime. This was not benefiting the children and such arguments were used to persuade parents to send their children away.

Although many children were happy and well looked after, some children suffered with families that did not care for them. However, it has to be considered that if they had stayed in the city, they might have died.

When all the arguments are considered, it can be seen that the idea of evacuation was better than leaving children in cities to be bombed.

# The Evacuation was Right

| | |
|---|---|
| **Opening sets out main topic and point of view** | During the Second World War many children were evacuated to the countryside. **This caused much controversy, but** on reflection it was the right thing to do. |

*Useful structure*

| | |
|---|---|
| **Main reason** | Long before war began, plans were drawn up to move children to the countryside **because** it was expected that the cities would be bombed. |

*Connective for providing reasons*

**Viewpoint – supported by extra ideas and reasons**

Parents did not have to evacuate their children, though there was considerable pressure. **It was considered** to be dangerous for children to be in cities. The bombing **would mean** that their lives were at direct risk. **Many also believed** that the young should be sent away because they might prove to be a distraction from the daily war effort. **It was also thought that** it was important to preserve the next generation.

*Useful clause*

*Causal phrase*

*Handy clauses*

**Providing a counter-argument by stating alternative view and then knocking it down**

**Of course,** some parents could not bear the idea of being separated and others needed their children to help with their daily lives. It has to be remembered that some adults could not cope alone as they had been bombed out. In these cases, some children ended up fending for the family and themselves, **little better than beggars on the street.** This often **led them into crime.** This was not benefiting the children and such arguments were used to persuade parents to send their children away.

*Sounding reasonable!*

*Showing the down side!*

**Further counter-view**

**Although** many children were happy and well looked after, some children suffered with families that did not care for them. **However,** it has to be considered that if they had stayed in the city, they might have died.

*Useful connectives*

**End – restating initial viewpoint**

When all the arguments are considered, it can be seen that the idea of evacuation was better than leaving children in cities to be bombed.

*Clear statement at end*

# Yes – UFOs Do Exist

Many people do not believe that UFOs exist. However, there are many reasons why this viewpoint can no longer be sustained.

Most people believe that the universe is endless. If this is the case, then this means that inevitably there must be life on other planets. It is obvious that other beings would be curious and attempt to make contact.

For years we have been sending radio signals deep into space and on several occasions an answering code has been returned. Although the significance or meaning of the return signal has not yet been deciphered, it is clear that something has been attempting to make contact with earth.

There have been so many recorded sightings by reliable witnesses, including the army and air force pilots, that the possibility of aliens can no longer be ignored. Many sightings are by ordinary people and not by 'cranks'. For instance, in 1961 Barney and Betty Hill reported being taken into a spaceship and tested by aliens to see how humans differed from their own species. Barney and Betty were put under hypnosis and had lie detector tests to try to ascertain the truth. Their story could not be disproved.

So, the arguments for UFOs are building up into an irrefutable picture. Indeed, those who do not believe are now considered to be a strange minority!

# Should Gold E. Locks Be Gaoled?

**This newspaper takes pride in presenting both sides of important issues. This week we are focusing upon the plight of Miss Gold. E. Locks who stands accused of breaking into the Three Bears' Cottage and breaking a number of items.**

Those who are campaigning for her release have put forward a number of powerful arguments that need to be carefully considered before making a decision about this girl's future. First of all, they make the valid point that Miss Locks was lost in a dangerous place. Many people would consider it wise of her to have sought shelter. Furthermore, she had not eaten for 24 hours and was on the edge of fainting from lack of food. Doctors have provided conclusive evidence that she would have also felt weary due to lack of food. Finally, it should also be remembered that Miss Locks is homeless and deserves to be supported in her desire to lead a better life.

On the other hand there are many who believe that the best treatment for this girl is to confine her to gaol. Those who take this position argue that she has broken several laws and the correct punishment is a gaol sentence. They also argue that if Miss Locks is dealt with lightly then it will only encourage others to break the law. Furthermore they suggest that a term in gaol would provide an opportunity for this girl to receive education so that she can support herself in the future. Finally, they state that the local area is suffering from a rash of homelessness – from vagrant pigs to others seeking their fortune. This should not be seen as an excuse for robbery.

Having viewed the matter with some care, the *Nursery Times* believes that Miss Gold E. Locks should be given a chance to put her life on a new footing. She has expressed her sorrow at the damage she has caused. A fitting punishment would be community service plus compulsory attendance at 'assertiveness for the homeless' so she can grow in confidence and discover how to get a job and pay her way.

Opening presents main theme

Reasons for

Reasons against

Conclusion with reasons for decision

# Should Gold E. Locks Be Gaoled?

**This newspaper takes pride in presenting both sides of important issues. This week we are focusing upon the plight of Miss Gold. E. Locks who stands accused of breaking into the Three Bears' Cottage and breaking a number of items.**

Those who are campaigning for her release have put forward a number of powerful arguments that need to be carefully considered before making a decision about this girl's future. **First of all,** they make the valid point that Miss Locks was lost in a dangerous place. **Many people would consider** it wise of her to have sought shelter. **Furthermore,** she had not eaten for 24 hours and was on the edge of fainting from lack of food. Doctors have provided conclusive evidence that she would have also felt weary due to lack of food. **Finally,** it should also be remembered that Miss Locks is homeless and deserves to be supported in her desire to lead a better life.

**On the other hand** there are many who believe that the best treatment for this girl is to confine her to gaol. **Those who take this position argue** that she has broken several laws and the correct punishment is a gaol sentence. **They also argue that** if Miss Locks is dealt with lightly then it will only encourage others to break the law. **Furthermore they suggest** that a term in gaol would provide an opportunity for this girl to receive education so that she can support herself in the future. **Finally, they state** that the local area is suffering from a rash of homelessness – from vagrant pigs to others seeking their fortune. This should not be seen as an excuse for robbery.

Having viewed the matter with some care, **the *Nursery Times* believes that** Miss Gold E. Locks should be given a chance to put her life on a new footing. She has expressed her sorrow at the damage she has caused. A fitting punishment would be community service plus compulsory attendance at 'assertiveness for the homeless' so she can grow in confidence and discover how to get a job and pay her way.

Title clearly states topic under discussion

Make the traditional sound modern

Sounding balanced

Connectives used to establish views

Connectives used to state opposing views

State own view clearly

Say why

# Was Jack Wrong?

By now everyone locally has heard the news that Jack has become wealthy beyond his wildest possible dreams. What many do not know is that this was brought about by stealing a golden goose from a giant. Should this sort of behaviour pass without comment? Here the *Daily Trumpet* sets out the arguments for and against the case. Once you have read the different viewpoints expressed below, use the phone line to vote for or against Jack. Next week we will publish the results.

Many people believe that Jack was in his rights to break into the giant's castle. They point out that the giant's wife hid him and therefore had taken his side. It should also be noted that Mrs Giant has recently filed a petition against her husband for cruel treatment. Some have stated in this paper that the giant had stolen the golden goose originally whilst he was pillaging the local area. Though it may be argued that Jack has therefore come in receipt of stolen goods, it could be said that the wealth the goose will bring to the area will be welcome.

Finally, it has to be remembered that Jack's new wealth will bring opportunities for work as he establishes his new business in the trade of magic beans, flying cows, walking-talking dishes and spoons plus a range of musical instruments that play by themselves while singing.

Taking the other side are all those who believe that although the giant is a disreputable character this does not make stealing a correct thing to have done. They believe that Jack has broken into the giant's house and stolen his golden goose as well as his talking harp. They claim that the harp called out to the giant during the robbery, thus demonstrating that it was reluctant to be taken. They argue that this is a clear case of harp abduction and against the laws of the land.

What do you think? We are withholding our views until you have cast your vote for or against the issue. If you think that Jack should keep his wealth because this will benefit the local area, phone 00998877. On the other hand if you believe that the goose and harp should be returned and Jack punished because he has committed a crime then phone 11223344. Results will be published in next week's Saturday edition.

# How to Trap an Ogre

Are you kept awake by the sound of ogres tramping through your garden?
Do you lie in your bed trembling at the sound of another car being squashed?
Do you awake to smashed walls and footprints in the flowerbeds? Do you live in
fear of what might await you round the corner? Do your knees knock at the
thought of a walk to the corner shop? If so, the likelihood is that you have an
Ogre in the neighbourhood!

Do not despair. Help is at hand. Ogres are not so hard to defeat, as they are rather
dim-witted. Read these step-by-step instructions and soon you too could be rid of
this terrible pest.

*What you will need:* a spade, a brown sheet, tent pegs, a sack of leaves, some
branches, plenty of soil, a large lump of meat.

*What you have to do:*

1. First, you must dig a very large and deep hole. This needs to be deep enough to
   hold the Ogre.
2. Secondly, you must cover the hole with a brown sheet that is pinned securely
   by tent pegs into the earth.
3. After that, scatter leaves, a few branches and enough soil on top of the sheet to
   cover it.
4. Now you have to tempt your Ogre by placing a large lump of meat on top of
   the sheet.
5. Hide nearby and wait.
6. Soon the tempting smell of the meat will reach the Ogre's nose.
7. Eventually, the Ogre will come along and try to get the meat.
8. In the end it will not be able to resist the food and therefore will fall straight
   into the pit.

**Important note**

An angry Ogre can be a frightening sight, so keep all little children inside. The
Ogre will try to escape so make sure that you do not go too near the edge in case
it can reach over the top. Some Ogres try to bargain their way out. They may sob
and weep and beg for their freedom. They may even promise you vast wealth, pretending that they know the whereabouts of a dragon's treasure trove. Do not be
fooled. Ogres are in the main very stupid and only think of eating and sleeping.

# How to Trap an Ogre

| | Title clearly states subject matter |

Are you kept awake by the sound of ogres tramping through your garden? Do you lie in your bed trembling at the sound of another car being squashed? Do you awake to smashed walls and footprints in the flowerbeds? Do you live in fear of what might await you round the corner? Do your knees knock at the thought of a walk to the corner shop? If so, the likelihood is that you have an Ogre in the neighbourhood!

*Opening establishes why reader might need to follow these instructions*

*Use of questions to draw reader into thinking about the need to follow instructions*

**Do not despair. Help is at hand.** Ogres are not so hard to defeat, as they are rather dim-witted. Read these step-by-step instructions and soon you too could be rid of this terrible pest.

*Short, punchy sentences for effect*

Colon

*What you will need:* a spade, a brown sheet, tent pegs, a sack of leaves, some branches, plenty of soil, a large lump of meat.

*What you need*

*Organise in list, in order of use*

*What you have to do:*

Use of 'you' addresses the reader, personalising instructions

*Numbers*

1.  **First, you** must dig a very large and deep hole. This needs to be deep enough to hold the Ogre.
2.  **Secondly,** you must cover the hole with a brown sheet that is pinned securely by tent pegs into the earth.
3.  **After that,** scatter leaves, a few branches and enough soil on top of the sheet to cover it.

*What to do – in chronological order*

4.  **Now** you have to tempt your Ogre by placing a large lump of meat on top of the sheet.
5.  Hide nearby and wait.
6.  **Soon** the tempting smell of the meat will reach the Ogre's nose.
7.  **Eventually,** the Ogre will come along and try to get the meat.
8.  **In the end** it will not be able to resist the food and therefore will fall straight into the pit.

*Use connectives to organise sequence*

**Important note**

An angry Ogre can be a frightening sight, so keep all little children inside. The Ogre will try to escape so make sure that you do not go too near the edge in case it can reach over the top. Some Ogres try to bargain their way out. They may sob and weep and beg for their freedom. They may even promise you vast wealth, pretending that they know the whereabouts of a dragon's treasure trove. Do not be fooled. Ogres are in the main very stupid and only think of eating and sleeping.

*Additional information*

# How to Catch a House Goblin

House goblins are a pest. They can become quarrelsome and noisy. Have you been suffering from sleepless nights? Do you wake to find that the fridge has been raided again? Do you put something down in one place only to find that seconds later it has moved rooms? Do you hear strange chuckling and gurgling in the early morning? Well, it sounds as if you might have a house goblin of the invisible variety living with you.

Read these step-by-step instructions for a goblin-free existence. Do not tolerate a lower standard of living. Why have your house mucked about by a greedy goblin? Get rid of it in eight easy moves. These instructions come to you courtesy of 'Remove It – the company that gets rid of goblins, ogres and all forms of unwanted ghouls'.

**Preparation time**: ten minutes.

**What you need**: plenty of courage, one bucket of superglue, shiny foil or object, a bag of flour, and a reinforced sack for transporting goblins.

**Suitable for:** dealing with one house goblin of moderate brain.

**What to do**:

a.  Begin by pretending not to notice the goblin. This will make it angry and less likely to spot any trap that you might set.
b.  First, spread a large quantity of superglue onto something glittery that the goblin might like to touch. A stone covered in shiny foil is a good idea, as the goblin will mistake this for a large diamond.
c.  Next, leave the object in an obvious place and pretend to be doing something else in an absent-minded manner.
d.  After that, turn your back, as this will tempt the goblin into mischief-making.
e.  The goblin will be unable to resist the temptation.
f.  Soon, the goblin will discover that it is stuck and make a terrible brouhaha.
g.  Once you have tracked down the noise, throw a bag of flour over it.
h.  Now you will be able to see the outline of the goblin. Place it swiftly into the sack and remove to another location at least ten miles away.

- Reminder: Wash hands thoroughly after touching goblins.
- Visit www.removeit/goblintraps.com
- 'Don't be a fool – get rid of that Ghoul!'
- Call REMOVE IT for help with the more stubborn ghost on 012345 6789.

# Stay Fit – Keep Healthy

Today sees the start of the new government programme for keeping the nation healthy.

Every year we spend millions of pounds on medical care for people who have lived unhealthy lives. If we could have a fitter nation, we would have more money to combat poverty in our society. So, prolong your life in these three sensible ways.

## 1. Eating healthily

Make sure that your diet contains a balance of carbohydrates (for energy). Protein is useful to ensure that damaged cells repair and can grow. Fats are good for energy in moderation. Vitamins will keep you healthy and fibre helps food move through the gut. Finally, drink plenty of water.

## 2. Take regular exercise

This helps to keep your muscles strong and your lungs working. It means that you will be well co-ordinated and unlikely to get fat as energy burns up excess food. It will also keep your heart working well.

## 3. Avoid unhealthy habits

Smoking, drugs and too much drinking damage your health and can be very dangerous, leading to an early death.

**Stay sensible – stay FIT.**

## TERM 3: **PERSUADE AND INFORM (FORMAL WRITING)**
(Easier)

# Stay Fit – Keep Healthy

Direct title – emphasises a positive

Opening – introduces topic

Today sees the start of the new government programme for keeping the nation healthy.

Every year we spend millions of pounds on medical care for people who have lived unhealthy lives. If we could have a fitter nation, we would have more money to combat poverty in our society. So, **prolong** your life in these three sensible ways.

Background information

Instructional tone

**1. Eating healthily**

Make sure that your diet contains a balance of carbohydrates (for energy). Protein is useful to ensure that damaged cells repair and can grow. Fats are good for energy in moderation. Vitamins will keep you healthy and fibre helps food move through the gut. Finally, **drink plenty of water.**

Present scientific knowledge to support views

Key arguments organised into three clear sections with subheadings

Instructional tone

**2. Take regular exercise**    Choose very clear headings to stay in the reader's mind

This helps to keep your muscles strong and your lungs working. It means that you will be well co-ordinated and unlikely to get fat as energy burns up excess food. It will also keep your heart working well.

Appeal to vanity!

**3. Avoid unhealthy habits**

Smoking, drugs and too much drinking damage your health and can be very dangerous, leading to an early death.

Appeal to their fears!

Punchy end – directive and appeals to being 'sensible'

**Stay sensible – stay FIT.**

# Rationing

## Important Information –
## for the sake of your country – 2 June 1941

Clothing is to be rationed as of today. It is of the utmost importance that we carry this out with determination, as it is crucial to the war effort.

On 3 February a list of items of clothing that have been rationed will be issued. This list will contain the maximum prices and should be adhered to rigidly. Please note that children's clothing will only be rationed after the age of four. Up to that age there will be no restriction on boiler suits, caps and clogs for infants. It is imperative that tomorrow's workers have a healthy start to life.

Styles will be restricted, in order to save cloth. Double-breasted jackets will not be issued and the number of buttons used in designing clothes will be limited. Designers have been asked to ensure that no extra details are added in order to make savings and to speed up and simplify production so that extra labour is not diverted into making clothes when it is guns that we need. For instance, stockings will not be on sale. If we make these sacrifices, it will save approximately £500 million within a year, which can be diverted to the war effort.

More importantly, we will be able to release many thousands of workers from the cloth mills so that they can work in munitions' factories. Many of the cloth mills will be converted so that they can produce weaponry and support the fight against the enemy.

Your support is necessary. All Britons must ensure that they are not wasteful. Please keep this information for your reference.

# Why Trolls are Dangerous

Trolls are considered to be the most dangerous creatures that roam the forests of this land. This can be explained in various ways.

Trolls have rather nasty eating habits that, generally speaking, involve the consumption of a large quantity of meat. This means that no live-stock or human being is safe when a troll is in the vicinity. Because trolls are meat eaters, human beings are not safe! Furthermore, trolls have no regard for human life. They see humans in the same light as any other creature so this means that they have no qualms at eating a child or adult! It is just like eating a hamburger to them!

Trolls are also fearless so they will not be concerned about any threat or attack. This is linked to the remarkably tiny brain that they have. Scientists have found it hard to actually discover a troll brain but believe that it is smaller than a peanut. This means that trolls are easy to deceive because they cannot think quickly. It also means that they do not easily get afraid so seem fearless in battle.

The one thing that trolls are afraid of is sunlight. They have been warned about this from birth by their troll parents. If they are caught in a sunbeam then this will result in the troll being instantly turned into stone. Unfortunately for the troll, the effect is lasting. If you ever see a rock formation that looks uncannily like something that once was living, you can be assured that it was a troll that was caught outside!

| Use 'How' or 'Why' | | Clear title that states what is to be explained |

# Why Trolls are Dangerous

**Opening – introduce subject**

Trolls are considered to be the most dangerous creatures that roam the forests of this land. This can be explained in various ways.

Generalised view

Use of causal connectives to explain how one thing leads to another

**Initial explanation with reasons**

**Trolls have rather nasty eating habits that, generally** speaking, involve the consumption of a large quantity of meat. **This means that** no livestock or human being is safe when a troll is in the vicinity. **Because** trolls are meat eaters, human beings are not safe! Furthermore, trolls have no regard for human life. They see humans in the same light as any other creature **so this means that** they have no qualms at eating a child or adult! It is just like eating a hamburger to them!

**Further explanation**

Trolls are also fearless **so** they will not be concerned about any threat or attack. This is linked to the remarkably tiny brain that they have. Scientists have found it hard to actually discover a troll brain but believe that it is smaller than a peanut. **This means that** trolls are easy to deceive **because** they cannot think quickly. **It also means that** they do not easily get afraid **so** seem fearless in battle.

Use of causal connectives

**End – final explanation**

The one thing that trolls are afraid of is sunlight. They have been warned about this from birth by their troll parents. **If** they are caught in a sunbeam then **this will result in** the troll being instantly turned into stone. Unfortunately for the troll, the effect is lasting. If you ever see a rock formation that looks uncannily like something that once was living, you can be assured that it was a troll that was caught outside!

Note sentence structure – good for explaining

# How to Care for Your Teeth

Teeth are essential for eating. Human beings eat both plants and animals and their teeth are especially suited to cutting, tearing and chewing their food.

The teeth at the back of your mouth are called molars and these are used for grinding food. They tend to be fairly large and flattish so that they can crush and chew food. Believe it or not, you have fangs called canine teeth that are used for biting into food and holding on! The flatter, sharp front teeth are incisors and are used to cut up food.

If we were herbivores like sheep and cows, we would have more molars for grinding food. If we were carnivores, we would have more canines for gripping and tearing meat.

As our teeth are important in helping us eat, we have to take care of them or eating might become difficult. Bacteria cause teeth to decay. If you eat sugary foods then this will be eaten away by bacteria, which forms a covering of plaque on the teeth. Plaque contains acid, which eats away the enamel that keeps teeth hard.

You can help prevent tooth decay. First you must brush twice a day to remove any plaque. If you drink water that contains fluoride, this also is believed to keep teeth strong. Do not eat too many sugary foods, as this is likely to cause decay. Finally, make sure that you visit a dentist regularly so that any signs of decay can be spotted and treated. So, stay healthy and look after those gnashers!

# Teachers' notes

## POETRY MODELS

### Pages 2–3: Poems using personification ('Oakridge Night' and 'The Day's Eye')

#### Reading
- Read through and discuss – likes, dislikes, puzzles, patterns.
- What effect is the poet trying to create – what mood do you think he was in when writing – and why?
- Identify use of internal rhyme, alliteration and personification. Discuss the effect personification has (it brings the scene alive . . .).

#### Writing
- The first poem is simple enough to emulate. Think of a place you know and jot down five or six things you can see, for example war memorial, trees, streets, moon, clouds. Then take each thing in turn and begin to build words around it, using personification, for example: 'The old moon grins . . .'
- 'The Day's Eye' (daisies follow the sun as it moves through the sky) has a tighter structure. This needs careful modelling but it can produce good writing. Instead of the sun as a subject, write about the moon. If rhyme is too hard for some, don't worry.

### Pages 5–7: Poems in different forms: riddles ('What Am I? and 'Who am I?')

#### Reading
- Read the riddles – look for clues. Note the acrostic pattern in the badger poem – usually acrostics make use of the first letter in each line to spell out the title – in this case I have used letters inside the poem, which actually gives the writer more scope.
- Identify and discuss the different images for the badger – and the plays on words for the tree riddle.

#### Writing
- Choose a subject to write a riddle about, for example an owl. Then brainstorm – what it looks like, what it does, what people think of it and so on.
- Use some of these ideas as clues to build a poem.

### Pages 8–10: Poems in different forms: haiku ('Seasonal Haiku' and 'Holiday Haiku')

#### Reading
- Read through the haiku and discuss – likes and dislikes. Which creates the strongest picture?
- Identify best use of language – how did the poet gain effects? What techniques are being used? Explain that these are written on the spot, notebook in hand – an attempt to capture the moment like a verbal snapshot.

#### Writing
- Do not worry about counting syllables – the seasonal haiku have a specific format to follow, e.g.
    Line 1 – season or month plus time of day
    Line 2 – what you can see
    Line 3 – what you can hear.
- Or encourage the class to use their notebooks to observe some small detail – something nobody else will have seen – and then capture it in a few words, using writing techniques.

### Pages 11–13: Poems in different forms: using everyday sayings ('An Odd Kettle of Fish' and 'The Poem Imagines it is a Horror Film')

#### Reading
- Read either poems and discuss the effect that the writer is using, taking everyday sayings literally. The second poem is somewhat bloodthirsty – you have been warned!

## Teachers' notes

### Writing

- Collect over time as long a list as possible of everyday sayings. This could be set as a homework task – for children to ask adults and others at home.
- Demonstrate how to follow the same format – and take the saying literally, e.g. 'His eyes shot across the room – drilling holes in the wall.' 'Her head was always in the clouds – it was very damp up there . . .'

## Pages 14–16: Poems in different forms: free verse ('Things to do Around Oakridge' and 'It's Early')

### Reading

- Read through and discuss – the list poem about Oakridge describes the sorts of things that my children have done around the village. 'Laggers' is the local name for the tiny paths that wind up and across the hill between houses. I have written this in four sections – one for each season.
- Discuss in relation to what they do and begin collecting a list – to be used in their own versions.
- 'It's Early' – discuss the most effective verses/lines – why?

### Writing

- Model a version of the Oakridge poem, using ideas based on what you used to do as a child.
- Or, use the model of 'It's Early' – perhaps focusing upon 'It's Late'. Make a list of sounds and sights that are heard late at night. Then, using all your poetic technique, model a few verses before they write, e.g.

      It's late –
      The moon yawns.
      Even the stars are weary.

      It's late –
      Cars cruise home.
      Cats wake and take on the streets...

## Pages 17–21: Short poem sequence ('Spanish Holiday' and 'South of France – Holiday Creatures')

### Reading

- 'Spanish Holiday' – read the sequence. Discuss preferences and children should justify by quoting.
- Look at different techniques, for example the one-line poems.
- 'South of France – Holiday Creatures'. Each of the mini-poems has a specific form – try counting the syllables to find the different patterns. They are all invented forms!

### Writing

- 'Spanish Holiday' – these are easy to imitate. Demonstrate how by taking a small detail and using poetic techniques to make something special. This is helped if you can take the class out somewhere, equipped with a notebook.
- To invent a form – try writing a mini-poem and then count the syllables and organise the lines to create a pattern.
- Sequences need to be rooted in the familiar, for example mini-poems for each season, each month, different animals, night creatures – try looking at animal books and writing a mini-poem for each illustration. The secret of this kind of writing is to observe very closely and carefully, to select words carefully, to use poetic technique and to compress the language – cut out any excess words.

## FICTION MODELS

## Pages 22–29: Narrative: defeating the monster ('Diving for the Brick' and 'Double Dare')

### Reading
- Both stories are based on 'defeating the monster' – in both cases the monster is within the character – fear.
- Diving – read and discuss – what sorts of fears do the children have?
  - How does the writer show how the main character and Petie feel?
  - What clues tell us about the teacher?
  - How does the writer make the reader feel sympathy for the main character?
  - Why do the class give so much praise?
  - Why do they fall quiet?
  - What has the main character learned by the end?
- Double dare – this story is also built around the motion of taking a dare that leads into difficulties.
  - Draw a graph to show Connor's feelings and how they change;
  - Why doesn't he want to take the dare?
  - Why does he accept it in the end?
  - Why does no one 'do the sensible thing'?
  - How could fear be like a 'quick-fire disease'?
  - Explain how he has changed and how do you know.

### Writing
- You could make a list of basic things that people are afraid of. Then select one and discuss a possible five-part plot:
  - Opening – reveal what character is afraid of.
  - Build up – put character in situation where they will meet fear.
  - Dilemma – they have to face their fear.
  - Resolution – they cope with it.
  - End – fear conquered.

## Pages 30–33: Narrative: a modern retelling from one viewpoint

### Reading
- Can anyone guess which stories these are retellings of ('Three Bears' and 'Sing a Song of Sixpence') – find the clues, for example 'The king was in his counting house'/'Dad was in his room on the computer'.
- What sort of character is Jules – what clues does the writer provide? Discuss different viewpoints in the retelling about the Jenkins family. What do Mr and Mrs Jenkins think of each other?

### Writing
- You could map out and then complete either story – or begin with a new version of a different tale, for example Miss Muffet – story about someone who is doing something they enjoy and then they get threatened by something and they flee.

## Pages 34–35: Narrative: summaries

### Reading
- Read through and discuss – who can guess which stories or rhymes they are based upon ('Billy Goats Gruff', 'Jack and the Beanstalk', 'Cinderella', 'Three Bears', 'Humpty Dumpty').

### Writing
- List other well-known rhymes and stories. Try to retell these in under 50 words.

# Teachers' notes

## Pages 36–39: Narrative: section of playscript

### Reading
- Read through. In threes/pairs act out the scenes provided – then improvise and extend.
- Note how the writer has to reflect character into what the actors say.

### Writing
- Either extend one of the scripts and complete the playscript or choose another well-known tale.
- It is worth 'boxing' the story up into scenes before writing to give shape to each scene or act.

## Pages 40–41: Narrative: reading log model

### Reading
- To revise you may wish to use some of the stories in term three this term.
- This could be used in any term – reading log entries need to vary and this is an example of an entry made after reading David Almond's book *Skellig*.
- The NLS list of suggested activities for reading logs can be obtained from any NLS consultant.

### Writing
- You could use the paragraph openers to act as prompts for a modelled version.

## Pages 42–47: Narrative: character story ('Kissing the Railings' and 'The Growler')

### Reading
- Read through the story and discuss:
  - 'Kissing the Railings' – what do you think the story will be about?
  - Collect clues about Kim.
  - What do you find out about Tom?
  - How does the end relate to the opening?
- 'The Growler'
  - How did they feel on the first day?
  - Why did they make a face at each other?
  - How does the writer make the reader think that the new teacher is wonderful?
  - How did the main character feel at the end?
  - What did he learn?
  - What advice would you give him?

### Writing
- These are character stories – based around a character flaw (always doing what you are told and singing badly!).
- Make a list of possible flaws, for example greedy, lonely, jealous, spiteful, etc.
- What sorts of problems would this lead you into?
- Get the children to draw on real-life experiences and fictionalise them.

## Pages 48–53: Narrative: finding story (reflection back in time) ('Top Cat' and 'Sam's Thief')

### Reading
- Read through and discuss.
- 'Top Cat' – why do you think they stopped when they heard the sound?
  - What do you think plaintive means?
  - What sort of person is Codger?
  - What do you think Codger thinks of the two children.
  - Hot-seat Codger and the boys.
  - Discuss the final paragraph.

# Teachers' notes

- 'Sam's Thief' – why do you think the writer uses the word 'moving' rather than a powerful verb in the third paragraph?
  - How old do you think Sam might be – any clues?
  - Why did he have to pause at the bottom of the stairs?
  - Why is the final paragraph just one sentence?
  - Look carefully for instances of sentence variation as this story is rich in them.

## Writing
- Both stories are built around the theme of 'finding' something.
- Try using a simple writing frame built around the same idea, for example:
  - main character goes out;
  - main character is en route;
  - main character finds something;
  - main character takes it home/looks after it;
  - ending.
- List possible ideas – you could find a creature, something precious, something someone else has lost, or you might find something abstract like courage or a friend.

## Pages 54–61: Narrative: traditional tale ('The Sack' plus two short sufi tales and 'The King and the Fisher Boy')

### Reading
- Read 'The Sack' and discuss.
- What is the theme: can anyone explain the plot in general terms in a few sentences, for example, someone who has suffered great misfortune, suffers another but has a reprieval and this therefore brings them joy – when in reality they are still in the same position!
- 'The King and the Fisher Boy' – why did the King behave as he did?
- Run an advice surgery for the King.
- What lesson was the hen wife trying to teach the King?
- What was the King's greatest flaw?
- Should he be King?

### Writing
- Take either of the little Hoja stories and retell them, elaborating.
- Or, take the longer tale about the fisher boy and try retelling it from the boy's viewpoint.
- Prepare for this by hot-seating the boy – or having him recount what happened in role to a television journalist.

## Pages 62–69: Narrative: fantasy ('Jack O'Lantern' and 'Thog's Journey')

### Reading
- Read through and discuss
  - 'Jack O'Lantern': what is the main character – where are the clues?
  - Why does he get scolded by his mother at the end?
  - Why was he sleeping in a wren's nest?
- 'Thog's Journey' – on a graph, chart Thog's feelings during the story.
- Why was he sent?
- What do you know about Olafson?
- Hot-seat either character about what happened.

### Writing
- You could write another adventure for Jack in which he nearly gets caught.
- Or, write the story of Thog's return journey.
- Prepare for this by sketching a story map and drawing in the terrain – then add on notes about what might happen.
- Reread the end of the story as there is a hint about the bee that will need using in the tale.

**Pages 70–72: Narrative: model plan for extended fantasy quest and template**

*Reading*
- Read and discuss the ideas.
- Turn the notes into an annotated story map.

*Writing*
- Demonstrate how to complete the template with fresh ideas.
- Use a story map to help – visual learners find story maps useful as visually they can see the whole plot in one go.
- A long story like this might be best in chapters – an incident per chapter.

## NON-FICTION MODELS

**Pages 73–75: Biographical and autobiographical writing ('Police Report: Recent Wolf Attacks' and 'The Wolf's Autobiographical Account')**

*Reading*
- Read through and discuss – noting the structure of the report.
- Use the structure as a template for future writing.
- Look at viewpoint – what do the police seem to think of the wolf?
- What is the wolf's view?
- What would granny say or one of the pigs?

*Writing*
- Prepare for writing by selecting another well-known tale and hot-seating characters or interviewing characters in role as television journalists.
- Put the wolf on trial.

**Pages 76–79: Non-chronological reports ('Catastrophes' and 'Amazing Animals')**

*Reading*
- Read and discuss content, noting extra points of information.
- Discuss how the author tries to draw the reader in and make the subject interesting.
- Tease out the basic structure:
  - opening – introduce subject matter;
  - paragraphs that focus on different aspect of the topic;
  - end: relate subject to the reader.

*Writing*
- Demonstrate how to write a report using the same framework. List possible topics – things that children in the class know about and are interested in.
- Before writing, use the OHP for children to make mini-presentations about topics that they know about and are interested in – one-minute talks.

**Pages 80–82: Non-fiction revision: letters**

*Reading*
- Read through and discuss – point out how humour can be created by using traditional material but treating it in a modern manner or setting.
- Use a grid to list the key complaints.
- Which ones are well supported with reasons or facts?
- Which is the better-argued letter of complaint?
- What will the reaction be of the recipient?

# Teachers' notes

- Hot-seat all those involved.
- Role-play a scene at the police station or a discussion between the two Ugly Sisters.

### Writing

- List well-known traditional tales.
- List ideas for possible letters of complaint, for example, pigs complaining about wolf, gingerbread man complaining about fox, goats complaining about troll – or troll complaining about goats!
- Before writing, hold a radio interview in which there is a phone-in and callers complain.
- Use key phrases from the two models that will be helpful when writing.

## Pages 83–85: One-sided argument ('The Evacuation was Right' and 'Yes – UFOs Do Exist)

### Reading

- Read either or both and discuss – take views and information from the class; most Year 6 children are interested in UFOs and some may have tales to tell!
- What is the view of the author? List key points being made.
- How does the author support views? Consider difference between opinion and fact.
- Which is a better argument, and why?
- Look at use of counter-argument to predetermine what the other side will say and how to knock it down without giving them a chance!

### Writing

- Choose another subject – possibly from the curriculum; for example, health issues in science.
- State viewpoint and then list key arguments – add in note form reasons and facts to help support views.
- Before writing, hold one-minute slots for children to propose their views.
- Demonstrate how to turn this into paragraphs, referring back to basic structure of models.

## Pages 86–88: Discussion and journalism ('Should Gold E. Locks Be Gaoled?' and 'Was Jack Wrong?')

### Reading

- Read through either and then discuss.
- If you look at both: what sort of papers are these editorials from; who might read them; how do they differ in style; what makes you think that; where are the clues?
- Note how a discussion that is balanced is different from a one-sided argument.
- List the points and decide whether the views are balanced, or if there is evidence of bias.

### Writing

- Make a list of possible topics and select one; for example, 'Should the porridge pot be used for the benefit of the community?'
- Demonstrate how to list reasons for and against a subject.
- Use this as a basis for a class debate.
- Then demonstrate how to turn notes into a discussion piece.

## Pages 89–91: Revision: instructions ('How to Trap an Ogre' and 'How to Catch a House Goblin')

### Reading

- Read through and discuss.
- Tease out basic pattern and language features – draw up a chart 'How to write a set of instructions'.
- Look at techniques the writer uses to make the reader want to use the instructions.

# Teachers' notes

## Writing

- List ideas for other topics; for example, how to trap a troll, how to look after a unicorn.
- Hold Agony Aunt sessions in which the Agony Aunt has to advise someone on how to look after a unicorn, etc.
- Demonstrate how to make notes and then write instructions.
- For fun, use fact boxes, adding in extra information.
- Look in real places to see how instructions are set out; for example, recipe cards from superstores.

## Pages 92–94: Persuade and inform (formal writing) ('Stay Fit – Keep Healthy' and 'Rationing')

### Reading

- Read through and respond – both of these relate to the curriculum.
- Look at how the writing is organised, listing structure – and then language techniques.
- Who wrote these and why? How do you know?

### Writing

- Organise a one-minute advert slot for pairs to present a persuasive and informative advert for a zoo park or some other such place.
- They should use the same sorts of devices; for example, punch statements, questions, alliteration, repetition, free offers, positive or negative language, slogans or catchy phrases.
- It helps to look in newspapers or magazines and to steal phrases from real adverts!
- Then use the persuasive devices in their own writing – as a pamphlet or letter.

## Pages 95–97: Explanation ('Why Trolls are Dangerous' and 'How to Care for Your Teeth')

### Reading

- One of these is based on the curriculum and the other is more imaginative.
- Identify the causal connectives and structures and list – these are essential for writing explanations – which hinge around explaining cause and effect.

### Writing

- You could use a curriculum area; for example, how friction works – or something imaginative; for example, why ogres eat so much.
- List ideas and use causal structures to create sentences that explain how things work or why things happen.
- It can help to write the explanatory sentences before the whole piece of writing.
- Consider too how diagrams usually help.

Printed in the United Kingdom
by Lightning Source UK Ltd.
107953UKS00001B/155-220

9 781843 120971